100 Tips For Blues

You Should Have Been Told

Also by David Mead available fromSMT:

10 Minute Guitar Workout
100 Guitar Tips
100 Tips For Acoustic Guitar
Basic Chords
Basic Scales
Basic Guitar Workout
Chords & Scales For Guitarists
Rhythm – A Step By Step Guide To Understanding Rhythm For Guitar

With Martin Taylor
Kiss And Tell – Autobiography Of A Travelling Musician

www.davidmead.net

Published by
SMT
an imprint of Bobcat Books Limited
14/15 Berners Street, London W1T 3LJ, UK

Exclusive Distributors:
Music Sales Limited
Distribution Centre, Newmarket Road,
Bury St Edmunds, Suffolk IP33 3YB, UK
Music Sales Corporation
257 Park Avenue South, New York, NY10010
United States Of America
Music Sales Pty Limited
120 Rothschild Avenue,
Rosebury, NSW 2018, Australia

Order No. SMT1045R
ISBN 1-84492-001-1
© Copyright 2003 David Mead
Author Image © Copyright 2003 Carol Farnworth
published under exclusive licence by SMT, an imprint and registered trade mark of
Bobcat Books Limited, part of The Music Sales Group.

Printed in the EU

A catalogue record for this book is available from the British Library.

www.musicsales.com

100 Tips For Blues Guitar

You Should Have Been Told

David Mead

ACKNOWLEDGEMENTS

My thanks, as usual, go out to Carol and all my family, friends and acquaintances who have to listen to me whining on about how writing books is actually a real job. Thanks, too, to everyone who has attended the various workshops, lessons and seminars I've given over the past few years and who have provided me with many of the questions that these books set out to answer.

Check out David Mead's web site at www.davidmead.net for information regarding workshops, gigs and books. If you have any questions arising from the material contained in this book, email David directly on info@davidmead.net

BOOK CONTENTS

CD CONTENTS

1 **Intro** – Tuning Notes
2 **Blues Harmony** – Blues Chord Voicings
3 **Blues Melody** – The Blue Third
4 **Blues Technique** – Vibrato
5 String Bending
6 Bending And Vibrato
7 Hammer-Ons And Pull-Offs
8 Slides
9 Style Analysis – Muddy Waters
10 Style Analysis – Mississippi Fred McDowell
11 Style Analysis – Elmore James
12 Style Analysis – Howling Wolf
13 **Accompaniment Ideas:**
    Intro Idea
    E Chord Idea
    A Chord Idea
    B7 Chord Idea

    Turnaround/Ending Idea – Full Piece, 'Kitchen Sink Blues'
14 Backing Tracks Intro/Goodbye
15 Backing Track 1 – 12-Bar Blues In E
16 Backing Track 2 – 12-Bar Blues In A
17 Backing Track 3 – I-IV Changes In C
18 Backing Track 4 – Riff Blues In E
19 Backing Track 5 – Slow 12/8 Blues In G
20 Backing Track 6 – Extended Key Change Blues In E, F♯, A and C
21 Backing Track 7 – Slow Song Form Blues With Chorus In G
22 Backing Track 8 – I-V Eight-Bar Blues (Including Diminished Chord On ♯4/♭5)
23 Backing Track 9 – 12/8 Minor Blues In C
24 Backing Track 10 – Jazz Blues In B♭

All highlighted items refer to chapter headings. All un-highlighted items refer to examples that can be found as illustrations within a given chapter.

CD produced and compiled/edited by Phil Hilborne. Mastered by Phil Hilborne. Recorded/mixed by Phil Hilborne at WM Studios, Essex, April 2003. Web/Info: www.philhilborne.com or www.philhilborne.co.uk.

David Mead used a Sid Poole Classic electric guitar and a Lowden F10 steel-strung acoustic guitar fitted with Elixir .12 steel strings. He also used Rode mics and Lexicon and Yamaha effects. He played all the guitars on tracks 2–14, lead guitar on track 1 and rhythm guitar on track 24.

Phil Hilborne played lap-steel guitar on track #1 and rhythm guitar on all backing tracks except track 24 and keyboards, strings and bass. He also carried out all programming/editing. Phil Hilborne uses and endorses PRS and Fret-King Guitars, Picato Strings and Cornford Amplification.

'Listen to the past… I've run into a lot of players in the last 10 or 15 years who didn't know where [the blues] was coming from. They thought it came from Jimmy Page, or they thought it came from Jeff Beck, or they thought it came from Buddy Guy, or they thought it came from BB King. Well, it comes from further back, and if you go back and listen to Robert Johnson, Blind Blake, Blind Boy Fuller, Blind Willie Johnson and Blind Willie McTell, there are thousands of them who all had something which led to where it is now. The beauty of it is that you can take one of those things and make it yours. But, by learning too much from the later players, you don't have that much opportunity to make something original. I listened to King Oliver and I listened to Thelonious Monk, Charles Mingus, John Coltrane, Archie Shepp… I listened to everything I could that came from that place that they call the blues.'
– *Eric Clapton, in conversation with David Mead in 1994*

INTRODUCTION

As far as the blues is concerned, believe it or not, some things are more important than pure technique. For instance, if you've got a kind-hearted woman, it's imperative that she has the meanest dog in town. You've got to be able to wake up each morning and find your shoes and it's absolutely vital that you show your jelly roll to anyone who displays even the slightest interest. After that, it's all plain sailing...

Seriously, teaching guitar styles that lack some form of acknowledged syllabus can prove to be something of a high-wire act on occasion. Central to this dilemma is how to get across some of the less tactile aspects of playing, those elusive things like 'feel' and 'motivation' being top of the list. The ticking mechanism behind the visible clock face, as it were.

As an example, I recently taught at a workshop in London where the subject was the 'unplugged' style of Eric Clapton, with particular reference to the CD of the same name. You're probably aware that, in this instance, there exists not only the CD of EC's performance, but also a video and a book of reasonably capable note-for-note transcriptions.

At the beginning of the seminar, I asked the assembled throng a question, which was basically, given that all this information is readily to hand, what's the problem? Surely everything one needs to know is there: a recording to listen to, a video to watch and check out, hand and fingering positions and, most conclusive of all, a book telling you where everything is located on the fretboard, along with helpful chord boxes and all.

After the chuckling had died down and everyone saw that I was, in fact, trying to make a serious point, I began to get some answers thrown back at me. Everybody agreed that, despite the facilities I had listed, they still considered themselves to be on very shaky ground. What's more, merely being told where to put your fingers didn't really seem enough; they felt they were still falling short of some sort of mark.

We agreed that this could be down to a lack of overall technique – being able to move your fingers fast enough or cleanly enough and achieving something of a pleasant sound at the same time. It's true to say that deftness on the guitar neck can be achieved over time with a fruitful practice routine in place – and a certain amount of self-discipline. But there is another, less obvious factor which acts as a barrier to progress.

Eventually, one student got to what I consider to be the crux of the matter: it's a matter of context. He was absolutely right: without an idea of a general context in which to place any new information, it's impossible to do anything other than to imitate rather than to innovate.

Nothing else would be possible without the necessary information that would give you the confidence to divert from the original path that was laid down for you by following the numerical instructions in the tab.

I likened it to learning a language solely from a phrase book: it would be possible to pick up some very useful titbits this way, but you'd flounder the minute anybody tried to engage you in conversation. For instance, you might be able to stride into a hotel in Tokyo and say, in fluent Japanese, 'Good morning,

I have reserved a room in the name of Evans,' but if the desk clerk did anything other than smile and hand you your key, you'd be in for something of a hard time. You simply wouldn't know enough about the language to diversify from your original intended path of conversation.

So it's context that I intend to address in this book. Filling in some of the background detail in this way will enable you to take the fullest possible advantage of today's easy access to study material.

During my tenure as a guitar-magazine editor, I had the great fortune to interview some of the truly great guitar players around. On this question of providing 'core learning' to a student, one of them said to me, 'It's easy to show someone a lick; you can write it out for them and, if they take it away and practise it for a while, they'll nail it. But the difficult thing is showing them where that lick came from. That's the trick: telling them what was in the guy's head when he played it originally.'

That, I believe is the most valuable course to take whilst examining the subject of blues guitar – to ask ourselves, 'Where does it all come from?'

Hopefully, I'm armed with enough of the answers to help you on your way towards achieving all of your musical goals – so let's get on with it!

David Mead
Bath, 2003

1 UNDERSTANDING NOTATION

'That was a strange sound, because that solo on *Another Brick In The Wall* was done through the desk; it was direct injected onto tape from the neck pick-up of an old Les Paul with P9os. But I didn't think it was biting enough, so we ran the tape out through a bit of wire and plugged it into an amplifier and put a mic in front of it. Then I fiddled around with the amp, got some volume on it, and then we mixed that sound and direct injected it back together.' *David Gilmour*

Music is a language and, as such, there are a variety of ways in which it tends to be written down. As far as the guitar is concerned, we have chord boxes, fretboard diagrams, tablature, standard notation and chord charts which are all used either together or individually to provide the overall picture of what goes where and when. If you are at all unfamiliar with any of these devices, then I would urge you to read this chapter before attempting anything else in the book.

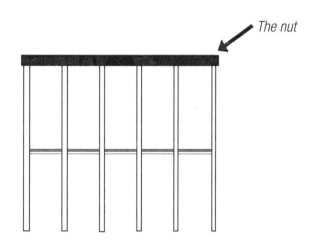

The nut

Chord Boxes

Chord boxes are snapshots of the fretboard which are usually used to show you where to put your fingers to form chords. The basic grid looks like this:

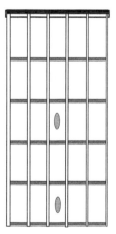

Here, you have to imagine that the guitar is facing you, with the thicker bass strings on the left. The thick line at the top of the diagram is known as the *nut* and marks one extremity of the guitar fingerboard.

Of course, not all guitar chords are down at the nut end, and if such a chord is shown in box form, it will be missing the thick line at the top. Instead, its location will be shown by a fret number, listed at the side like this.

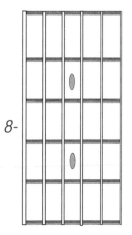

8-

15

In the previous diagram, for instance, you would be expected to line everything up on the eighth fret.

The actual finger positions are shown by black circles on the strings. So, if we wanted to write down a chord of C major, it would look like this:

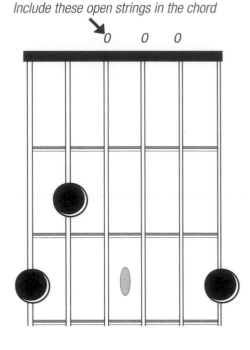

Include these open strings in the chord
0   0   0

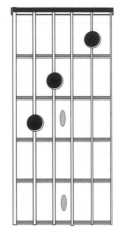

Not all guitar chords use all six strings of the guitar, and so when you're expected to miss some out, a little letter 'x' is put over the relevant string.

In the above chord of G major, the D, G and B strings would be sounded along with the fretted notes to produce the chord.

When a barre chord is notated, you'll see a thick black line across all of the strings, like this:

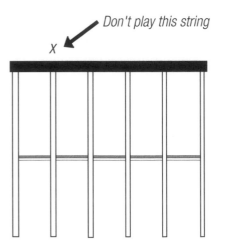

Don't play this string
X

On the other hand, if you're expected to sound the open strings within the chord, this is indicated by placing a letter 'o' over the string or strings concerned.

The black line indicates that the first finger is placed across all six strings and the rest of the fingers form the other notes in the chord. A number by the barre tells you the exact location.

8-

Fretboard Diagrams

These are similar to chord boxes but are used to illustrate information like string relationships or scales.

Once again, if the action takes place down at the nut end of the guitar fretboard, this will be indicated by a thick black line, as before.

So, if an exercise incorporated two notes on the G string – say, frets five and seven – things would look like this:

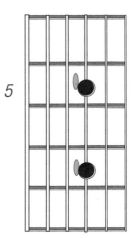

This form of diagram gives us a sort of bird's-eye view of what's going on down on the fretboard and is handy

for giving an overall impression of scale shapes like this one:

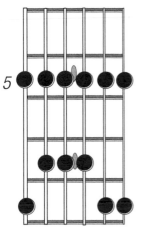

The guitar is a 'shape friendly' instrument and so it's common and useful for a lot of information to be recorded this way.

Tablature

Tablature, or *tab* for short, is probably the most precise method for transcribing melody and harmony for the guitar. It's a dedicated system, meaning that it really works only on the guitar and that other instrumentalists can't be expected to understand it (especially drummers).

Tablature first saw the light of day about 400 years ago, when it was used to notate lute music. There are examples of tablature from this period in many museums across the world today, so go and take a look sometime if you're interested in our ancestral heritage as guitarists!

Tab fell out of favour because it was such a confining system – other instrumentalists couldn't fathom it and, more importantly, guitarists or lutenists couldn't communicate with players of other instruments via a written language. So the more universal standard notation won the day and, despite being far more vague on an instrument where most notes have more than one location, guitarists have just had to toe the line for ages.

The rebirth of tab came along hand in hand with the resurgence of interest in the instrument at around the '60s and '70s. At first it was inaccurate and ambling at best, but by the time the '80s were in full swing, tab had once again become the way to understand guitar music more fully. Now, you can pretty much rely on the fact that, somewhere on the planet (and hence somewhere on the Internet), just about any solo, guitar part or whatever is available in this form.

Tablature starts off as six horizontal lines, each representing one string of the guitar, with the bass E at the bottom.

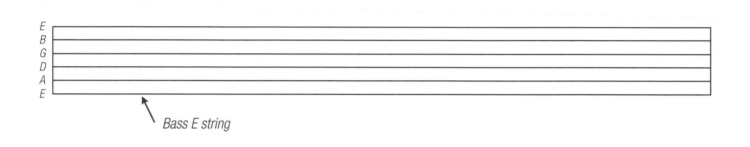

Bass E string

Fret locations are shown as numbers on their appropriate lines, like this:

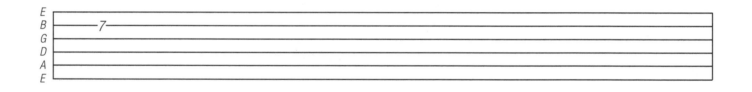

The tab above is telling us to play the note located at the seventh fret on the B string. So, you can see what I mean about being a precise and dedicated form of notation for the guitar. If someone is telling you which string to play and which fret to put your finger on, you're not lacking any information at all (except 'Why that note?' – something of an author's message for this book).

Chords are shown as vertical columns of numbers, like this:

If the previous diagram looks a little perplexing, you might welcome an accompanying chord box:

Both the diagrams are telling us to play the chord C major. Arguably, the chord box is a tad clearer, but you're likely to come across both out there in the field, and so it's best to familiarise yourself accordingly.

Believe it or not, that's about all you need to know about reading tab for now. It's such a direct and easily manageable system that you can go a long way on the information above. However, there are a couple of extra things that are bound to crop up along the way and so we might as well look at them while we're here.

Bends

When a bent string must be indicated in tab, it is written out like this:

The idea here is that the ordinary number in the tab tells you where the note is to be bent from and the note in brackets is the pitch you're meant to bend the string to. For instance, in the above example you would carry out your bend on the seventh fret of the G string and bend it until you reached the pitch of the ninth fret. Whilst you are still perhaps a little unsteady on your feet where string bending is concerned, this gives you the opportunity to play the note you're bending towards first, keep the pitch in mind and bend the string until the desired pitch is reached.

It sounds a lot more complicated when you write it down, but I'm sure that a few experiments will find you bending strings like a pro!

Slides

As we'll see later on in the book, sliding is an essential aural trademark of the blues and a good way of getting from one scale position to another. When a slide is to be included in a phrase (that means it's actually heard, as opposed to a silent position change), it's notated like this:

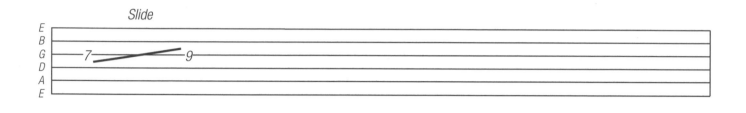

If you place your finger on the seventh fret of the G string once again, strike the string with the pick and slide your finger to the ninth fret, you should be able to hear a continuous note literally sliding between the two pitches.

There are various other signs that appear in tab, but these two are the important ones as far as the task in hand is concerned. Anything else will be explained in the text.

Standard Notation

Because of its universal status in music, standard notation is altogether a tougher nut to crack than its tab counterpart.

This form of written music is very old, too, going way back to the 14th century and possibly beyond. Obviously, it would be almost impossible (and largely irrelevant) for me to try to teach you how to read music here and now, but I think it's important that you are equipped with a few reference points, at least. For

instance, at one time or another, you're going to come across some music without tab, in which case the very basic ability of finding out which note is which is going to come in handy.

The first task we'll undertake is that of learning to recognise the grid system used by standard music notation. Unlike tab, we've got five lines instead of six, with a funny looking squiggle at the beginning.

The first thing to learn here is that the five lines are called a *staff* or *stave* (very few things in music have only one name!). The squiggle at the start of the line is actually a deformed letter G. Once upon a time, a very baroque-looking capital G was written at the beginning of the staff to indicate that this was the *treble* or *G clef*. As we'll see, it actually wraps its tail around the line in the music that represents G – but let's not run before we can walk...

There are quite a few different clefs in music, but the guitar is notated on the treble clef, and so we really don't have to worry about the others too much.

Next job is to learn where all the notes are. If you cast your mind back to music lessons at school, you might recall being taught how to remember the names of the notes on the lines of the staff. It generally went

something like 'Every Good Boy Deserves Favour', although the F has evolved a whole set of alternatives like 'Fruit', 'Fireworks', 'Football' or, in the case of one particular music teacher I once knew, 'Flogging'!

Whichever way you choose to remember it, the lines read E G B D F from bottom to top.

The names of the notes on the lines...

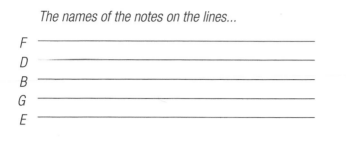

The spaces are a lot easier to remember, in that they actually make up the word 'FACE'.

In fact, I think the best way to remember things is that the notes start at E on the bottom line and read alphabetically upwards: E F G A B C D E F. Everybody

...and in the spaces

knows their alphabet and, putting aside the question of good boys deserving fruit, favours or football, you always end up working it out this way around, anyway.

The example below shows you where you can find this particular array of notes on the guitar. Your first task is merely to familiarise yourself with the look of the notes on the staff and their locations on the guitar fretboard.

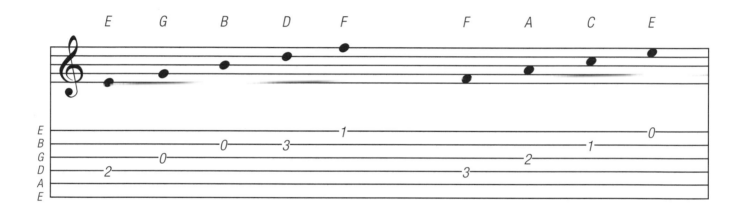

Perhaps you can see already why it is that tab wins all the prizes for instant translation into music as far as the average guitar student is concerned...

But, if tab has any shortcomings at all, the first of these would have to be that it contains no reference to rhythm. It's fine if you want to play something you may have heard on a record – all you've got to do is listen to the correct rhythm or phrasing and attempt to imitate it. After all, you already know which notes to play, and so adding this 'final touch' shouldn't be too difficult. But what happens if you're trying to work something out that you're not too familiar with and a copy of the relevant CD isn't to hand? That's where standard notation can come to the rescue and provide an answer.

As I've already said, I haven't got the room to give you the whole story about reading this form of notation – it would be a book in itself. (In actual fact, I've written

a book called *Rhythm: A Step By Step Guide To Understanding Rhythm For Guitar* – also published by Sanctuary – which addresses reading rhythmic notation, so if you want some more answers they are to be found right there.) But here are some of the basics...

Rhythmic Notation

Everybody has a built-in sense of rhythm. We are all sensitive to the 'pulse' of music and feel moved to tap our feet or somehow move in time to music. Understanding how this vital musical element is written down is really all about maths, albeit on a very elementary level.

Almost every piece of music has a 'beat' to it, and when it's written down we divide the staff into rhythmic cells called *bars* using vertical dividing lines known as *bar lines*.

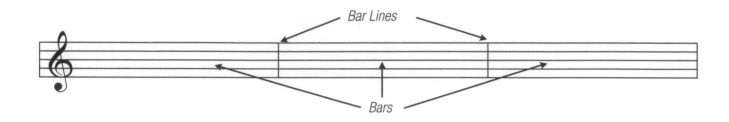

Bar Lines

Bars

Each bar contains the same number of beats and is mathematically identical in rhythmic value to every other bar in the piece (unless noted). This just means that everything is a little more organised and easier to read.

To tell us how many beats there are present in each bar, we check out the *time signature*, which is at the beginning of a piece, just after the clef.

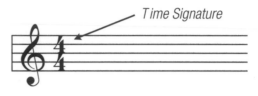

Time Signature

In the case of the example above, the fraction-like figures tell us that the prescribed rhythm here is to be 4/4. This means four beats to the bar, each beat being a *quarter note* or *crotchet*.

All we've got to think about for now is how a bar of 4/4 is counted, because this is a vitally important fundamental to get established before we can take understanding rhythm any further.

Take a look at the next example. Here, you have a situation where there are four beats to the bar with a counting regime outlined above. Learning to count and practising regularly with a metronome or drum machine is vital in helping you to achieve a sense of rhythm, and so it's a very good thing to take some time out in order to make sure you've got the idea well and truly in your head.

After establishing a solid 4/4 beat, working out the possibilities is really down to elementary mathematics.

The beat can be split in half, which gives us *eighth notes* or *quavers*:

Or it can be divided into four, which gives us *sixteenth notes*, or *semiquavers*:

It can even be split into three equal parts, known as *triplets*:

So a table of note values would look like this:

One quarter note is equal to...

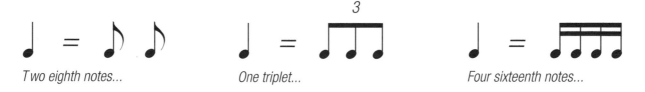

Two eighth notes...   *One triplet...*   *Four sixteenth notes...*

There are other horrors in store for the music reader, of course, but these are things that all fall outside our main brief – that of learning to play the blues. You'll be able to find out all about things like rests, key signatures, ledger lines, dotted rhythms and all the other items from music's curiosity shop in most elementary music handbooks. But I hope I've been able to shed a little bit of light in the music-reading room and that you will be able at least to work a few things out this way around.

Chord Charts

As you might suspect, a chord chart notates the chords contained in a piece of music without any reference to the melody. So, what you're seeing is a series of chords laid out so that they give you all the information you need – like the number of beats per bar, for instance.

Chord charts look something like this:

‖ C7 / / / ‖ C7 / / / ‖ C7 / / / ‖ C7 / / / ‖
‖ F7 / / / ‖ F7 / / / ‖ C7 / / / ‖ C7 / / / ‖
‖ G7 / / / ‖ F7 / / / ‖ C7 / / / ‖ C7 / G7 / ‖

This is a very basic blues in C. The forward-slash marks after the chord symbols tell you that you're expected to play each chord four times in each bar. As an example, in the first bar you'd play C7 four times. The very final bar is split equally between two beats of C7 and two of G7.

Even if this sounds a little confusing at first, you'll find that using this system becomes pretty much second nature before long. As well as being easy to understand, it's also a great way of getting across to other performers some basic information about a song, such as chord arrangements and so on, without needing to go the whole way and write out something far more detailed.

That just about covers everything we'll be looking at in the upcoming chapters of this book. If there are any departures from the norm, I'll explain it somewhere in the accompanying text.

2 HOW TO USE THIS BOOK

After years in the guitar-teaching biz, it occurs to me how similar the act of learning music is to that of learning a language.

The first language we all learn is our native tongue – and we learn it via a purely aural mechanism. We're immersed in it every day of our early lives, picking things up word by word, gradually beginning the work of assembling a vocabulary that will enable us to communicate with the world at large. It's here, too, that we take on board the various rules of grammar, way before we're taught to understand what's going on later in the school classroom. Over the years we continually learn about syntax, colloquialism, speech patterns, inflection and so on in such a way that, eventually, we are able to communicate almost anything. In fact, we learn how to express verbally the things that we merely feel. Some people, of course, take this basic skill further and become poets, writers or whatever.

This is almost exactly the same way that a lot of folk music is learned, too – and I would certainly define the blues as being a folk music at its birth. Songs would be learned almost subliminally, handed down from one generation to the next, picking up different nuances here and there as different musician's personalities became stamped upon them. Such was the evolution of early blues.

Today, of course, things have moved away from this purely aural process to far more academic means. We have tabbed solos, music books, videos, DVDs, CD-ROMs and so on which are dedicated to learning the guitar in all its stylistic forms.

This, to my mind, is more like learning a second language, where the same rules of grammar, syntax and so on are principally book-learnt. Again, we begin with basic vocabulary, slowly building up to longer and longer phrases, with total fluency as an eventual and often very distant goal.

It's an intense and difficult course – seemingly far more difficult than learning our first language ever was – and many fall far short of their fluency objective. This explains why so many have to resort to shouting and pointing when their knowledge of a language falls short of fluent communication!

I see a lot of musical shouting and pointing at guitar seminars where certain skills have not been developed to the point at which anything else becomes possible, and so a system of hit-and-miss randomising is called into action, usually in the hope that it will pass for real music!

This book sets out to place the task of learning to play blues guitar in an overall context, by tracing the development of the music back to its roots and, as Eric Clapton says in the quote at the beginning of the book, listening to the past.

I would encourage you to read Chapter 3 on blues history and take note of the recommended listening list at its end. This will serve to give you an idea of the overall development of the music and help fill in some of the blanks along the way.

Next, progress with the harmony and melody chapters, taking note of Chapter 6, 'Blues Technique', along the way. Each chapter offers you a practice plan whereby you will learn things in the correct order with a set of reasonable goals to lead you forward without ever losing sight of the fluency objective.

Patient, persistent practice are the keywords here – have fun working through the exercises in the book and playing along to the backing tracks on the CD, too. Good luck!

3 TIMELINE: A LITTLE BLUES HISTORY

Whether or not you get too much from this chapter depends on how much you want to regard Eric Clapton's advice on listening to the past at the beginning of the book. During his developing years as a player, Clapton studied the blues with an almost insatiable appetite. In 1994, when I had the pleasure of engaging him in conversation on behalf of the UK's *Guitarist* magazine, he went on to elaborate, 'I spent all of my mid-to-late teens and early 20s studying the music. Studying the geography of it, the chronology of it. The roots, the different regional influences and how everybody interrelated and how long people lived and how quickly they learned things and how many songs they had of their own and what songs were shared around. I mean, I was just into it, you know?'

Eric is far from being unique, too; many of the players I've talked to over the years have expressed the same desire to research their subject and can talk authoritatively about the origins of the music. Of course, we could argue that such research could be career-motivated and not quite so fundamental to the idea of playing blues guitar either casually or, at least, semi-professionally. Fair enough, but I know myself that there is considerable value in considering the past with an eye on the future. I've made the journey myself, raking out historical recordings from the early 20th century and learning from what I found. I've also taken it upon myself to point students in that direction, and they have generally been surprised at how much it has helped them put what they're learning into some sort of historical perspective.

Got Those Jam-Session Blues...

As an illustration of how even a little bit of revision can be of benefit from possibly the simplest point of view, I generally ask my students early on in a seminar what they think would happen if I said we were all going to jam on a blues in A together. There's always some uncomfortable shuffling in seats at this point, but, after a while, we tend to agree on at least a couple of things:

- it would probably be a 12-bar blues;
- it would probably default to a shuffle rhythm;
- it would probably depend on an accompaniment figure like the one below.

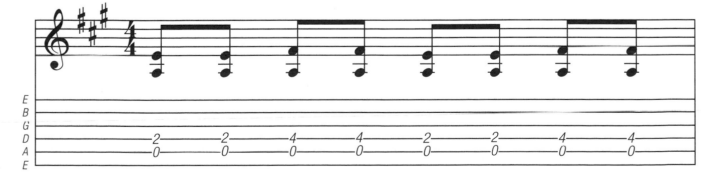

There is an unofficial 'number four' that states:

- it could easily end in complete chaos.

But we'll let that one ride for a moment...

It's at this point that I launch into my history lesson, telling people that what we were destined to jam on is merely a sort of default blues – a cliché which is almost completely non-representative of what the blues is all about. In fact, a 12-bar shuffle is really only the tip of an enormous iceberg and not worth much at all, unless the information it puts across is considered within a far larger context. When this is the case – and only when this is the case – can you even begin to think of yourself as a fully fledged blues musician. I'm even prepared to say that if you actively seek out some of the blues music that inspired today's great exponents of the form, you'll rarely find that familiar *chung-chunga* shuffle rhythm at all!

So, my advice here would be to scour record libraries, the Internet and just about every other resource centre you can think of to find recordings by some of the players we're going to be looking at during this chapter. Moreover, listening to anything that helps you form some kind of historical perspective about the music you've chosen to specialise in is going to help you on your own particular journey of discovery.

In The Beginning...

Nobody knows exactly what the earliest blues actually sounded like. Electronic recording began only during the 1920s, from a commercial point of view, and it is only from this period that we can be sure of our ground. Everything that went before, in terms of the archaeology of the blues, is down to educated guesswork and the odd fact gleaned from history books. It's usually not music-history books, either; the most interesting facts come from many diverse sources. Books about the history of the American slave trade of the 18th and 19th centuries; the American Civil War; the emancipation of the slaves; the subsequent withdrawal of the political rights – and many other rights, for that matter – of the emancipated slaves; the history of the American railroads; and the

migration from the rural south to the industrial north of the USA are just some of the sources that blend together to give us a better picture of how the blues came into being. In these terms, the earliest recordings actually appear quite late in the overall time scale of the music's history.

Of course, we're not destined to study the early development of the blues at such an intense level here; I'm interested only in giving you a workmanlike knowledge of early blues to the extent that it might prove fruitful to your own endeavours – and, at the same time, offer a platform from which you'll be able to extend your research, should you wish to do so. So, relax, sit back and enjoy the ride. I think you'll find it fascinating.

Born In Slavery

I think that just about everyone reading this knows that the blues started with the slave trade. This was the abominable trade in human life that saw the tribes of the west coast of Africa plundered by unscrupulous traders and their cargoes of men and women taken across the Atlantic, their journey ending in the slave markets which fed the cotton fields and farms of the American Deep South. The conditions in transit were deplorable and the death rate high – and, once landed and sold, the rate of work expected from the slaves was cruel, generally lasting from the first light of day until dark.

Steps were taken to ensure that all vestiges of the slaves' original African culture were smashed: families were broken up and all instruments that were considered to be 'tribal' – drums, for instance – were forbidden. One thing that was positively encouraged, however, was singing. The landowners had the notion that a singing slave is a happy slave, and so field songs, work songs and so on were allowed. In this, the slaves were able to continue at least something of their African musical heritage.

If any synchronised movement was called for – chopping, rowing and hammering, for instance – then singing was used to make sure everyone's movements were properly co-ordinated. Usually, this would take the form of 'call and answer', where one phrase was sung by the leader and an answering phrase was chanted by his team. This is a device which has survived even until today; call-and-answer phrasing is still a common form in blues solos. Originally, a

chopping song would be phrased so that the blow of the axe took place on the first beat in the bar, as shown below:

Even this concept survives today in contemporary blues. Think of how many blues phrases actually omit

this beat both lyrically and instrumentally. This is where it started.

Later on, in the early 1900s, the call-and-response form of blues vocals became an acknowledged part of performance, the responses often being improvised by either a second vocalist or even a group of vocalists. (Incidentally, one performer who explored this particular style of the blues was Pearly Brown. It's worth trying to track down some of his very rare recordings to check out the style for yourself.)

So, even then, improvisation was becoming a part of the blues's overall canon – a thing which is reflected in other forms of 'folk' music across the world, Spanish flamenco being a good example.

Of course, there are many more musical aberrations that have stood the test of time and become embedded in the blues to the extent that they make up a vital part of its unique form today. To go into all of them here would be a serious sidetrack – remember, we're really interested only in a sketch in order that the past helps us to obtain a better understanding of the present and offers, perhaps, a few new directions for those guitarists who are inclined towards researching the subject more fully.

If you're curious, there are lots of books available

that delve deep into the comparisons between early blues and West African tribal music. One of the best I've found is *Early Jazz* by musicologist Günther Schuller. It's also worth checking out Paul Oliver's excellent series of books on the development of the blues, particularly *The Story Of The Blues*.

That's Why They Call It The Blues

Apparently, the blues, or 'having the blues', was first referred to in print as early as the 1860s. We can assume that the expression had long since acquired meaning by this time, and the concept of actually 'singing the blues' was only just around the corner, chronologically speaking. But, as I have said, much of what led up to the earliest actual recordings of the blues is open to conjecture, and so it's convenient for us to jump forward at this point to the turn of the century, at which point history becomes far more sure-footed.

I'm missing out a fair slice of history here – we're leapfrogging over the American Civil War, the end of slavery and the beginnings of the great migration from the south of the USA to the industrial north. However, there is very little here that had too much of an influence on the music itself, at least as far as we are concerned, with our rough sketch. We pick up the pieces once again with the earliest recordings of Charley Patton in around 1929.

Charley Patton was born in 1891 deep in the Mississippi Delta and grew up on a farm with his parents and 11 brothers and sisters. He was to become a famous guitarist and vocalist, singing, we can assume, music handed down from the previous generation of bluesmen and embellished by Patton himself. His recorded work gives us an insight into the stage of development that the blues had reached at the turn of the century. It also lays a solid foundation for what was to follow.

Despite the fact that Patton is often heralded as the earliest of the recorded blues guitarists, a young man by the name of Sylvester Weaver actually beat Patton to that claim by some six years. Weaver was an accomplished guitarist, capable of playing ragtime as well as blues. His 1923 recordings for the New York-based Okeh label include both a blues and a guitar rag and are well worth tracking down, alongside Charley Patton's early works, as part of the basis for an essential timeline for blues guitar.

Listened to today, Weaver's style certainly goes a long way towards dispelling the myth that the early blues guitarists were poor musicians who were only able to tune the instrument to a single chord and use some sort of slide to work the changes. What is perhaps even more surprising is the influence of ragtime on the nativity of what we now recognise as blues. It is thought that ragtime and very early jazz influences gave some kind of rhythmic shape to the more meandering forms of vocalised blues from the same period. But here, possibly more than at any subsequent period, the influence is audible: the music is a blend of blues, ragtime and jazz, and so guitar styles mimicked this. A few of the early guitarists had previous experience in playing the banjo – if you think back to the minstrel shows I'm sure we've all heard about, it's obvious where exactly this might have come from.

Apparently, the banjo was sufficiently alike some of the African stringed instruments – most notably the banjo – to be readily taken up by some of the original slaves. It's certainly possible that some of the early guitar fingerpicking styles were overlaid on top of the original banjo picking techniques.

The Birth Of The 12-Bar Blues

Another blues pioneer from roughly the same period as Charley Patton and Sylvester Weaver was WC Handy, who is thought to have been the first songwriter to have used the term *blues* in a song title, as far back as 1912. It was also during the first ten years of the 20th century that the 12-bar structure for the blues was solidified as pretty much the standard form for some early blues. Certainly, the blues songstress Ma Rainey used the 12-bar form in much of her work and is widely credited for its ongoing popularity. Later on, in the late 1920s, she was to hand the baton to Bessie Smith, who became the most popular female blues singer of her time.

So, taking even the most casual overview of the period between 1900–30, it's possible to see (and, for that matter, hear) the individual elements of the music coming together to form the nucleus of what we know today.

Another factor certainly worth considering is that the onset of recording meant that the individual blues musicians were able to hear each other's work and become influenced by what they heard. Furthermore, the Depression during the 1920s saw a boom in the entertainment industry in the United States (it was the same era that gave birth to Hollywood), and so there was certainly no shortage of recorded material from which to draw.

The same period also saw the introduction of Prohibition – basically, a ban on the sale of alcohol – and this gave birth to underground, illicit drinking clubs that offered essential live platforms to both jazz and blues musicians of the period. In this way, the stage was literally set for blues guitar to bloom and develop in the hands of those who were eager to explore this exciting new medium for themselves.

Amongst the guitarists and singers from the late 1920s who were definitely an influence on their fellow bluesmen was Blind Blake. Blake hailed from Tampa, Florida, and his guitar style shows the still-prevailing influence of ragtime on the blues.

Put into a historical perspective, it's easy to see how this rag/blues style of playing was also influential upon early jazz guitar. Listen to the playing of Lonnie Johnson from this period and you'll see how at one point it was difficult to tell the two styles apart, with some jazz tunes being referred to as 'blues' and yet bearing all the up-tempo fire that would later be taken forward by post-war players like Charlie Christian. Back in the early 1930s, however, the two styles were very much seeds in the same pod.

As well as being a pioneering composer and performer, Charley Patton also taught guitar, and one of his pupils was the legendary Son House.

Eddie 'Son' House was first recorded in 1930, at the beginning of the decade that was to end in World War II – which, as we shall see, proved to be an important marker in the blues timeline.

Another student of Patton's was 'Bukka' White, who, it turns out, was a cousin of BB King. White came from Aberdeen, Mississippi, and achieved a reputation as a fine slide-guitar player. BB King claims that his cousin was a significant influence on his own early playing, describing his vibrato as 'the sweetest thing this side of heaven'.

As the recording industry switched into high gear during the 1930s, recordings by players like Mance Lipscombe, the Reverend Gary Davis, Big Bill Broonzy, Blind Boy Fuller and Scrapper Blackwell all helped to establish the blues within its own stylistic boundaries. Lipscombe's blues were out of rural Texas; Gary Davis turned out to be an excellent guitarist and is well worth studying even today; Broonzy learned blues from an uncle who had been a slave and went on to produce his own signature style of jive blues; Blind Boy Fuller was an exponent of rag/blues guitar; whilst Scrapper Blackwell's recordings with pianist Leroy Carr are of great historical interest.

All of the musicians listed above are well worth checking out in the interests of exploring early blues styles and providing yourself with a context in which to place your own music. There are plenty of compilation CDs on the market that feature these guys and others, and so your research is not going to be expensive. (In fact, in your interests, I've just put on my hat and coat and wandered around the record shops of Bath in the act of convincing myself that the above statement is true. It is – there is a positive embarrassment of early blues compilations available as I write. I was even tempted by a couple myself!)

Despite the fact that perhaps some of the names we've been considering during our whistle-stop tour of the early blues scene might not be too familiar to you, I'll bet that you've heard of the next gentleman. Ladeez an' gentlemen, the King of the Delta Blues Singers: Robert Johnson.

The Devil Has All The Best Tunes...

'If the Robert Johnson "Crossroads" thing had happened in Great Britain, it would have been, "I went down to the roundabout..."' *Bob Brozman*

To be honest, I think that Johnson's revered position as chief architect of modern blues is a little exaggerated. If you do your homework and check out recordings by some of the people we've been considering, you'll see that, if anything, Johnson merely sums up pre-war acoustic blues. Far from being the originator he is often hailed to be, Johnson had several things working in his favour. First of all, he was undoubtedly a very, very talented guitarist and singer. Secondly, he had the advantage of having the myth of 'meeting the Devil at the Crossroads'. Thirdly, he joins artists like Hendrix, Stevie Ray Vaughan, John Lennon, Charlie Parker and others like them in the fact that he died young and in particularly tragic circumstances.

First things first, though. I'm counting on the fact that you've all heard the legend of Robert Johnson, the Devil and the Crossroads. If not, here's a very brief overview. (This story has been repeated many times and it's available in just about every book ever written on the subject of the blues, so please forgive me if I skim over the details here.)

Basically, the story goes that young Johnson was not such a good guitar player until he mysteriously disappeared for a while. When he returned, playing so well it literally startled everyone he knew, he did so with stories about going down to the Crossroads (mythologically speaking, a place that has had a lot of supernatural significance attached to it in the past) and starting to play his guitar. After a short time, the

Devil turned up, Johnson handed him his guitar, the Devil then tuned it and handed it back, making the bargain that Johnson was granted his legendary chops on the instrument in return for his soul.

This particular myth was enriched by the fact that Johnson's repertoire of songs contained 'Crossroads Blues' – which tells the story itself – and other haunting gems like 'Hellhound On My Trail', 'Me And The Devil Blues' and 'If I Had Possession Over Judgement Day'.

As it turns out, the Devil didn't have long to wait for delivery of Johnson's soul because he died in very mysterious circumstances at the tender age of 27. The story goes that Johnson was an unrepentant womaniser, often favouring the 'already married' variety, and this led to his downfall at the hands of a jealous husband who had access to both poison and whisky – a lethal combination that brought about the great Delta bluesman's end.

So much for the legend. What about the music? There's no doubt that Robert Johnson's sole recording sessions in November 1936 and June 1937 have left us with the most complete picture of a Delta bluesman's work. Doubtless Johnson had learned from his forebears, taking from many sources, mixing and matching and generally making things his own. That was the way things were done back in the days before copyright laws came in and complicated matters! But the performances are absolutely stunning and vital to every blues student's understanding of the music in general. A bluesman who turns his back on Robert Johnson is like someone studying '60s pop music and ignoring The Beatles. Listen to his guitar accompaniment on '32–20 Blues' and how it unwittingly blazes a trail for blues-guitar rhythm that would outlast the 20th century.

Another thing that Johnson's recordings do is neatly round off the pre-war blues period. Things were set to change over the next few years, but the recorded history of the blues underwent another period of silent running during the war due to the shortage of shellac, used in the production of those early discs. The record industry had to limit severely the number of releases they made during this period, and blues was considered to be low a priority. Things consequently went quiet, at least from a commercial point of view.

The Electric Age

'I kept a guitar by the bed with the radio turned down real low, nobody would hear it except me, and every time a guitar would come on and you'd hear something, you'd grab the damned guitar right then and get as near to what you heard as you can.' *Buddy Guy*

If World War II marks the end of the classic acoustic blues era – which I suppose, very loosely speaking, it does – then post-war blues took on an almost completely different guise. For a start, somebody had come up with the idea of amplifying the guitar...

North To Chicago

Back in 1941, Robert Johnson was dead and gone, but his legend lived on – and it had just reached the American Library of Congress. This organisation had the splendid idea of recording indigenous American folk music in the field and would send their emissary, Alan Lomax, out into the countryside armed with portable recording gear to capture as much of this precious material as he could before it vanished into history. In this way, they managed to build up an incredible resource and deserve the thanks of every music researcher in the world.

On this occasion, Lomax went looking for Robert Johnson, but whereas details of the bluesman's legendary skills had begun to filter through, details of his death hadn't and Lomax looked like he would be coming up empty-handed. As luck would have it, he found a young farm worker who had learned Johnson's repertoire note for note – his name was Muddy Waters. Still working on a plantation, Muddy recorded a couple of numbers for Lomax before doing a full session later on. These would become known as Muddy's *The Plantation Recordings* and are well worth tracking down in order to hear some pre-Chicago Muddy Waters.

Until I heard this story, one thing had always puzzled me about this particular period of blues history. I knew that part of Robert Johnson's legacy was that he went on to influence the next generation of blues players – particularly Chicago blues – but I couldn't fathom how much of a direct link there had been between Mississippi in the south and Chicago in the north. This was despite tales of the great move north made by many workers in the south owing to various economical disasters like the dustbowl, invasions of boll weevils (nasty little cotton-eating insects that were themselves the subject of many a blues song) and the ever-increasing effects of the Depression.

Now, however much of an influence Johnson had on the young Muddy, it is beyond doubt that Waters took something of the King of the Delta Bluesmen with him when he migrated north in 1943.

Electrification

When he arrived in Chicago, Muddy Waters worked hard on his performance. Taking manual jobs by day, he would play in small venues at night, gradually alerting people to his own particular blend of blues.

I suppose the thing that we most associate with Muddy is the electric guitar, which he switched to the year after reaching Chicago. There was much speculation about exactly why Muddy chose to change over to the new electric breed of instrument, but when someone asked him, he replied, 'I just needed to be heard!' The truth was far away from any folklore; he was playing larger and larger clubs – and adding musicians to his group – and no one could hear him play on acoustic guitar. An uncle came to the rescue and gave him an electric guitar and the problem was solved. Blues had turned another corner.

Waters' reputation grew and grew. He managed to secure a recording contract with Chess, a Chicago-based label put together by brothers Phil and Leonard Chess in 1949. The Chess label attracted the talents of many of the Chicago bluesmen – and early rock 'n' rollers, too – in the form of Sonny Boy Williamson, Bo Diddley and Willie Dixon, the latter acting as in-house songwriter and talent scout for the label. Later on, during the mid '50s, Chuck Berry would be added to the roster and another dramatic stylistic change would come about.

With the war well and truly over, the record industry was back to full production and blues recordings started to thrive once more. Muddy Waters' first hit, 'I Can't Be Satisfied', laid the foundations for what was to become known as Chicago Blues.

One of the principal changes evident here is that,

whereas pre-war acoustic blues had been mainly solo guitar players and singers – with maybe the odd duo – Muddy's Chicago blues laid down the foundations for the blues ensemble: variations upon the 'guitar, bass, drums, piano and harp vocals' line-up grew up everywhere and the new sound was an instant hit with the record-buying public.

The influence of Muddy Waters' music was profound. Today he is hailed as the Father of Chicago Blues, and rightly so, his 'children' in this respect being artists like Buddy Guy and Otis Rush. Of course, '40s Chicago wasn't the only place to give blues a home; over in Detroit, John Lee Hooker was creating a sound that would become his own, too. John Lee's style of playing and bassy vocal delivery went on to influence artists as diverse as Carlos Santana and Led Zeppelin.

'With John Lee Hooker you'd never know when he was going to change chords! He'd sing until he got tired and he'd start playing guitar and then he'd do that until he got tired and then he'd sing again! It wouldn't be what you might think of as being on metre, and so you really had to listen and be real careful, because John Lee was going to play his stuff and you better fit into it because he wasn't gonna fit in with you!' *Johnny Winter*

Other notables from the same period include Elmore James, who is reputed to have played with Robert Johnson back in his Delta years and certainly made Johnson's 'Dust My Broom' his own; T-Bone Walker, the Texas-born bluesman who settled on America's West Coast and took electric blues guitar technique two or three steps further; and BB King, an acolyte of T-Bone's who was born in Mississippi and went on to spend most of his life touring and playing the blues with bands of all sizes. BB took guitar vibrato to new extremes, using it as an expressive tool to dress up his fiery guitar lines – his album *Live At The Regal* is another on our list of essential blues guitar recordings.

The British Invasion

This side of the war, the history of blues is obviously more recent and better documented than the far-off days of the Mississippi Delta. Many more recordings were made and thankfully, through the media of TV, video, CD and latterly DVD, much of this material is in plentiful supply. Names like Howlin' Wolf and Big Bill Broonzy are not so strange to the current generation of blues guitar enthusiasts, their historical imprint far better preserved than that of their forebears who worked and played 70 years earlier.

Surprisingly, though, blues remained on the secrets list on both sides of the Atlantic until the mid 1960s. In the USA, blues was still looked on as being 'black music' and was, as such, destined to be available only to black people. A few white artists caught on, however – it was said that Elvis Presley got a lot of his vocal style from listening to black blues and rock 'n' roll artists, for instance.

The effect of musical segregation was set to continue, until a small collective of blues enthusiasts in Britain became captivated by this 'new' music being imported by a few specialist record shops in the UK. Blues found itself on British radio, too, with the odd Howlin' Wolf tune cropping up in between the pop hits of the day.

At the dawn of the 1960s, Hank Marvin and The Shadows weren't the only influences beginning to inspire small boys everywhere to ask for a guitar for Christmas; so too were highly prized recordings by Muddy, T-Bone, Big Bill Broonzy...

Among these small (and, let's face it, not so small) boys were the likes of John Mayall, Eric Clapton, Peter Green and, collectively, The Rolling Stones.

As far as the British blues boom – or whatever you would like to call it – was concerned, it seems to have comprised small pockets of individuals who latched onto the music and prized it over anything else. From the number of people I have talked to who were involved in this particular era themselves, it seems that you were considered to be a bit of an oddball if you didn't enjoy the current pop scene in Britain or, for that matter, subscribe exclusively to the rock 'n' roll fraternity. So if you were lucky enough to run into someone else who happened to be into blues, there would be an almost instant bond.

Of course, many of these acolytes played instruments and, hence, bands were put together to play this exciting new music.

Some of the more famous blues enthusiasts of the early '60s include the gentlemen named above, who would slave to work out the music for themselves on their chosen instruments. If you were a guitarist and could string a few Freddie King licks together, you instantly became a member of an elite and quite likely to be hunted down by various groups of the day. Clapton told me during the previously mentioned interview that you didn't even have to be very good – you just need to be able to find your way through a few tunes and, if you were any good, you could play gigs and earn some money. He went on to say that there weren't too many of them around at that time and so it was easy to rise to the top.

Certainly, there was a time when the live music scene was far healthier than it is now and you could go around a town like Richmond in Surrey after dark and find several bands playing – and some of them would be playing blues-orientated music. And if you were a musician who didn't happen to be playing that night, the chances were that you would be out and about checking out the musicians who were. So, if you happened to find The Rolling Stones playing in a pub, it wasn't too much of a shock to find Eric Clapton and Jeff Beck sitting in the audience. Superstardom for all concerned was still a few years away; in those days it was just an exclusive little club.

'I started playing in 1956, which was also the year that Elvis Presley became famous, and I'm from the part of the world where country music is pretty successful. So when I was just nine years old, I was already a rock 'n' roll, country and western, blues fanatic. That's pretty unusual, but it gives me a broad sense of musical roots.'
Rick Derringer

Naturally, it didn't take the British record industry long to skim the cream – literally, in one case – and start recording bands like The Yardbirds, The Animals, Alexis Korner, The Rolling Stones and John Mayall's Bluesbreakers. The Beatles were blazing a trail and various companies took the chance that this particular form of music was going to be around for a couple of years and they wanted a piece of the action.

Then, in 1966, the world was changed once again when Clapton joined John Mayall's band and together they produced *John Mayall's Bluesbreakers* – or, as it is known colloquially, the '*Beano*' album in deference to the fact that Clapton is seen reading a copy of the popular children's comic on the album sleeve, totally oblivious, it seems, to the fact that he was writing history. Thus we reach another of our essential albums…

The '*Beano*' Album

'What I'm trying to recreate is the emotional experience that I got when I heard all of those songs. They took me to some beautiful place and made me feel better, or gave me cold chills when I heard them, so I try to make that happen again by playing them.' *Eric Clapton*

The 'Beano' album was one of the most influential British blues albums of its time. Prior to this, no one had heard a Les Paul used as angrily and as bitingly. In order to get the sound he heard on albums by Freddie King, Clapton went into the studios and – to the general dismay of the recording engineers present, who were more used to recording classical music – turned his Vox AC30 amplifier up full. 'I thought the obvious solution was to get an amp and play it as loud as it would go until it was just about to burst,' he told me in 1994. The resulting guitar sound turned heads and became the model which others became set to recreate.

Alas, Eric's tenure with The Bluesbreakers was a short one, but the next guitarist to step into his shoes was to prove almost as influential. Peter Green was aware that he had quite an act to follow, but he did so by applying the law of opposites; where Clapton had been an angry young bluesman, Peter's cool melodic lines, drenched in reverb and sometimes with almost superhuman sustain on his Les Paul sat perfectly in the music landscape provided by Mayall's smokey blues.

Enter Hendrix

Around this time, another revolution took place. The Animals' bass player, Chas Chandler, came across a young guitarist in the States who was just tearing the place up – but without much of an audience. Chandler decided that this particular guitarist's blues-powered rock would go down better in Britain, and so the legend of Jimi Hendrix was born. Hendrix was not known as being a blues guitarist *per se*, but the blues certainly touched everything he played and no overview of the blues would be complete without reference to the man. If you've never owned a Hendrix album before, you should at least seek out Jimi's various recordings of 'Red House'.

There's little doubt that without Hendrix there wouldn't have been The Cream – not in quite the same way, in any case. Clapton's next venture after leaving John Mayall was to explore improvised blues at a much higher decibel level, and although the band weren't what you might think of as being a 'pure' blues outfit, Clapton's solo on Robert Johnson's 'Crossroads Blues' from Cream's live *Wheels Of Fire* album is pretty much mandatory fare if you like your blues served hot and rocky.

Between The Cream and Jimi Hendrix, the UK achieved a salesman's dream; we literally sold the US something that was actually theirs in the first place. White awareness to blues grew exponentially on both sides of the Atlantic and suddenly the surviving pioneers of the classic blues establishment such as Muddy Waters, Howlin' Wolf, BB King and John Lee Hooker found themselves playing to bigger and bigger audiences.

Blues To Date

Of course, that's far from being the end of the story: players like Stevie Ray Vaughan, Robben Ford, Eric Bibb, Johnny Winter and many others like them continue, through their recordings, to influence contemporary blues styles and ensure that the music continues to evolve. But their story is comparatively recent history and doesn't really belong here.

The main reason for going back to the beginning of the 20th century was in order to set up a timeline that would enable you to learn the blues from each of its separate periods of development and, in doing so, become a complete blues guitarist. Remember, it's all a question of context.

Recommended Listening

I'm not giving you a shopping list here! Remember that there are loads of compilation albums that will allow you to sample many of the players I've been talking about in one place, and if what you hear there interests you, other paths of research will open up for you quite naturally.

I've highlighted several albums I think are essentials in order that your overview on the blues should be complete. These represent my own tastes, so I trust you'll forgive me if I seem to have missed a few. In my defence, I'll say that a complete blues-guitar discography would fill a book in itself – all I'm doing here is encouraging you to sample some of the music you might have otherwise overlooked.

Look for compilations or historical archives featuring the recordings of:

- Pearly Brown
- Charley Patton
- Sylvester Weaver
- WC Handy
- Ma Rainey
- Bessie Smith
- Blind Blake
- Lonnie Johnson
- Son House
- 'Bukka' White
- Mance Lipscombe
- Reverend Gary Davis
- Big Bill Broonzy
- Blind Boy Fuller
- Scrapper Blackwell
- Robert Johnson
- Muddy Waters – *The Plantation Recordings*

Meanwhile, here are some electric-era players who are well worth tracking down for study:

- Muddy Waters

- Sonny Boy Williamson
- Bo Diddley
- Willie Dixon
- Buddy Guy
- Otis Rush
- John Lee Hooker
- Elmore James
- T-Bone Walker
- BB King
- Howlin' Wolf
- Big Bill Broonzy
- Freddie King
- Albert King
- Alexis Korner
- John Mayall
- Eric Clapton
- Peter Green (with John Mayall and early Fleetwood Mac)
- Jimi Hendrix (particularly 'Red House')
- Johnny Winter
- Stevie Ray Vaughan
- Robben Ford (particularly *Talk To Your Daughter*)

Finally, here's a brief list of selected recordings. Keep your eyes on library record sections, second-hand shops and Ebay!

- Blind Blake – *Ragtime Guitar's Foremost Picker*
- *Blind Blake Vol 3*
- Reverend Gary Davis – *Blues And Ragtime*
- *Big Bill Broonzy And Washboard Sam*
- *Robert Johnson – King Of The Delta Bluesmen* (available in many forms, with a varying number of tracks. Fanatics should aim for the double CD, which contains the out-takes as well!)
- Muddy Waters – *The Plantation Recordings* (Chess)
- BB King – *Live At The Regal*
- *John Mayall's Bluesbreakers With Eric Clapton*
- John Mayall's Bluesbreakers – *A Hard Road* (with Peter Green)

4 BLUES HARMONY

'Don't just solo – get the groove going!' Bob Brozman

Bob Brozman is absolutely right – too many guitarists enter into blues thinking that it's about soloing, and by doing so are missing an essential point. Developing a good sense of rhythm and a solid ear for harmony are vital tools for the soloist and not just the accompanist.

The fact is, I suppose, that no one wants to consider themselves as being classed as a rhythm guitarist. It still smacks of incompetence or second-class citizenship in the world of guitar playing. But, in all the workshops I've ever taken, one fact remains constant: many students there are capable of playing a nice solo when it's their turn to have a stab at it, but virtually none of them has much of a clue about getting a groove going.

It's a fact that a guitarist in the professional field is judged not only on his ability to fly around the neck of the guitar, playing all the deep emotional stuff, but also his ability to keep a solid, interesting rhythm part going. And by the phrase 'interesting rhythm part' I don't mean a succession of barre chords with a straight 4/4 *chunk*. There's far more to it than that, as we're about to see...

Delta Harmony

If we keep to the theme of this book and start learning about blues harmony from the early days of the music, a few things will become apparent very rapidly:

- Blues is essentially a 'folk' music, meaning that it wasn't put together by students of some Mississippi-based music academy with a guitar in one hand and a rule book in the other. And so, for the most part, we're dealing with some pretty straightforward stuff. Blues only began to get fancy when the jazz boys started to have a go themselves a bit later on.

- Nothing that happened in the early development of the music did so because it was 'musically correct'. Mostly, it was a case of the musicians concerned trying to make the sounds they heard in their heads – music that had been handed down for generations using a purely aural means; learning by ear and playing by ear. A great deal of the nuances implanted into blues from the onset might have been purely subconscious on the part of the musicians involved. These people might have been obeying a set of culturally established impulses – known as *enculturation* by people who enjoy using long words.

- The notion that most of the early blues players merely tuned their guitars to a chord and used a bottleneck, slide or knife to change chords is wrong. Blues might not have had the savvy that it does now, but it wasn't musically backward, as reference to any of the 'early blues' CD compilations currently on the market will verify.

- A blues isn't necessarily a 12-bar in the accepted teenage-jam-session sense of the word – it can be 8 bars, 16 bars, 10 bars or even 32 bars with a chorus, intro and coda.

Chord Voicings

So, armed with all this, where do we start? We start with chords – but, more specifically, chord voicings. Practically everyone who has had any experience with the blues will know that its principal chord form is the dominant seventh – you can't move for the things – so, a blues in C at its most basic would look like this:

```
|| C7 / / /| C7 / / /| C7 / / /| C7 / / / |
| F7 / / /| F7 / / /| C7 / / /| C7 / / / |
| G7 / / /| F7 / / /| C7 / / /| C7 / / / ||
```

Now, this doesn't usually happen in music – you don't normally see chord arrangements made up entirely from seventh chords; technically, it's not musically sound to do so. Dominant sevenths have their job to do in music and, because this job is so specific, there's usually only one per key. So, if we actually 'corrected' the blues above, we'd end up with this:

```
|| C / / / | C / / / | C / / / | C / / / |
| F / / / | F / / / | C / / / | C / / / |
| G7 / / /| F / / / | C / / / | C / / ||
```

Even after this academic makeover, it still wouldn't quite follow all the correct procedures. In strict music terms, the dominant chord precedes the tonic – in this case, the C chord, like this:

```
| G7 / / / | G7 / / / | C / / / | C / / / |
```

If you play through the above example, you'll probably agree that it sounds properly punctuated, musically speaking. The important relationship here is between the G and C chords: the G7 signposts the C. And that is precisely why dominant chords feature in music; they act as signposts, imply movement and so on. So, in that way, having a daisy-chain of them in a blues doesn't make a lot of musical sense.

Dominant chords are renowned for sounding 'unfinished' – for instance, which sounds better in this example, A or B?

A

```
| G7 / / / | C / / / |
```

B

```
| G7 / / / | C7 / / / |
```

I've got a sneaking suspicion that you would probably agree that A sounded more 'complete' than B. To be really heavy-handed and prove the point with another example, it's a little like ending a sentence with a comma rather than a full stop.

The cat jumped on the table,

...as opposed to...

The cat jumped on the table.

The first example implies that, after having jumped on the table, the cat concerned did something else, whereas the full-stop version is complete and gives the impression that this was the end of the story.

It's exactly the same with music: dominant sevenths are almost like commas – unfinished, implying that the tale is not yet done – and major chords are rested and final, just like a full stop.

So, why did blues adopt this contradictory behaviour in the first place? If you look back to points 1 and 2 a few paragraphs ago, you'll probably guess at the answer: it just sounded better that way.

The I-IV-V Sequence

It is thought that the whole idea of chord arrangements was introduced to the original forefathers of the blues via Western folk songs – which are renowned for their C-F-G-type chord arrangements. Most folk-style songs are built on three chords from any single key and are known to musicians everywhere as 'I-IV-V' arrangements. These 'one four fives' get their name from the fact that it's always the first, fourth and fifth chords in any one key that the songs are based upon. Take a look below:

```
C  D  E  F  G  A  B  C
1  2  3  4  5  6  7  1
```

If you check out where the first, fourth and fifth notes lie in the C major scale above, you'll find that they correspond directly to C, F and G and, more specifically, the chords built upon these particular notes. What's more, this is a trick that works in every key:

$$
\begin{array}{ccccccc}
G & A & B & C & D & E & F\sharp & G \\
1 & 2 & 3 & 4 & 5 & 6 & 7 & 1
\end{array}
$$

Once again, the first, fourth and fifth notes in the G major scale turn out to be G, C and D. And if we turn these notes into fully fledged chords, look what we end up with:

Gmaj   Cmaj   D7

If you look at a few simple folk-type arrangements, you're bound to find these chords cropping up pretty much everywhere.

So, after running across some simple folk tunes which were either thought to be American (naturally) or even European (especially Irish) in origin, and being based upon straightforward I-IV-V arrangements like the ones above, when it came time to writing their own music, a great many of the blues' architects adopted the I-IV-V progression but turned each of the chords into dominant sevenths, merely because it sounded better that way around.

Nothing more to it than that. Theorists and ethnomusicologists (I love that word) alike agree that the blues was the bright spark that was born of the collision between Eastern and Western music traditions, and this is a very good example. Many books have been written over the years in the interests of supporting this theory, so we're not going to go into any more detail here. I'm not pretending to be an ethnomusicologist, however much I like introducing the word into casual conversation...

The CAGED Concept

So, for the sake of stressing a point, we're agreed that it's dominant-seventh chords that feed the blues and give it its plaintive, yearning and unfinished sound – I hope – because the next task in this quest to make our blues playing become 'real' is to see where to go next.

It's probably true to say that if you asked the

average guitarist to play a series of dominant-seventh chords, he'd choose one or other of these following two shapes to voice each chord:

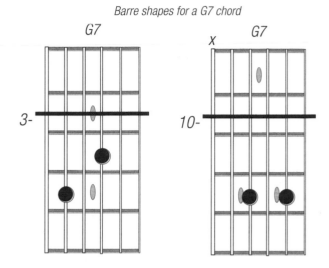

Barre shapes for a G7 chord

After all, why not? These two particular barre shapes are economical and they both sound fine – but they don't sound 'right' in very many cases. And so, in order to bring about the necessary degree of accuracy, we need to look a bit further into seventh chords in general – not so much what they are, but what voicings you have at hand as worthy alternatives.

So how many different types of seventh chord are available? Well, loosely speaking, there are just five different shapes:

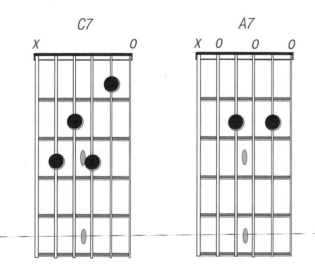

The first two of our five shapes

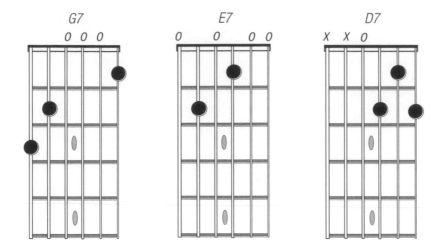

The remaining three shapes

Above, you have dominant sevenths based on the well-known nut-position chords C, A, G, E and D, and believe it or not but nearly every other chord voicing in this book is based upon one of these shapes. This might be surprising, but it's true and is based upon an ages-old device called the *CAGED system*, which first saw the light of day during the '50s and '60s.

Basically, the fretboard is split into these five shapes and all the various chord and scale shapes are built up around them, as illustrated in the diagram on the next page, which shows you how this process starts, using the basic shapes stretching up the fretboard in the key of C.

Making It Real

So, taking a look at our dominant seventh shapes, we've agreed that we know these two:

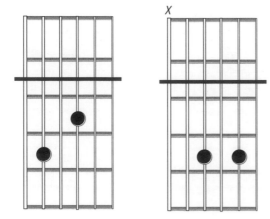

And so we can afford to disregard them for the time being and concentrate our efforts instead on the following two:

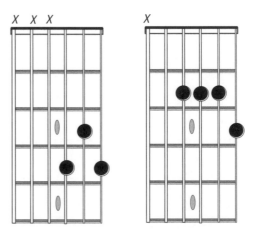

Now, let's imagine for a moment that we have before us the chords to a blues in E – a very common early-blues key. If we were to write out the progression, the chord chart would look like this:

‖ E7 / / / | E7 / / / | E7 / / / | E7 / / / |
| A7 / / / | A7 / / / | E7 / / / | E7 / / / |
| B7 / / / | A7 / / / | E7 / / / | E7 / / / ‖

Try playing through the arrangement above using the chord shapes that you might normally be drawn to when faced with having to play something like this. I'm guessing that the ones you instinctively pick will probably be these, all played down at the nut in the open position:

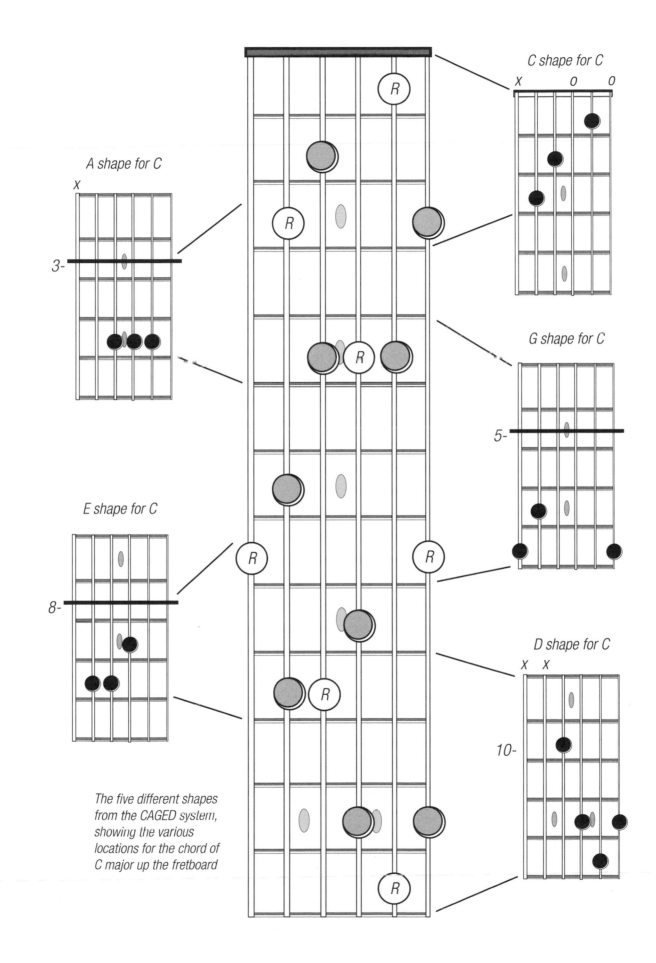

A shape for C

C shape for C

G shape for C

E shape for C

D shape for C

The five different shapes from the CAGED system, showing the various locations for the chord of C major up the fretboard

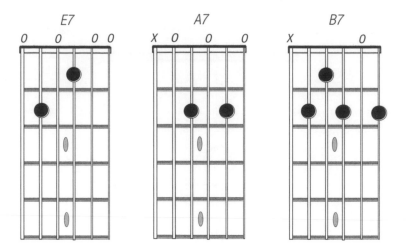

Now play through it again, but this time using different voicings for the chords. Try these chord shapes instead:

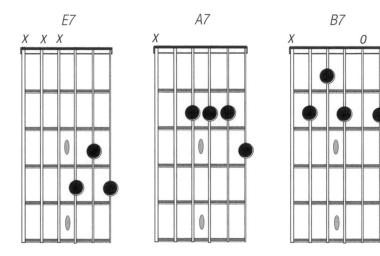

Both examples sound OK, but the second one sounds more 'authentic' as far as the ambience of early-blues guitar goes. All we did was substitute other seventh-chord voicings and look what a difference it made.

Looking even closer, some of the time it was standard practice to use this chord voicing for both the A and B chords:

We can even stretch this voicing to the E if need be:

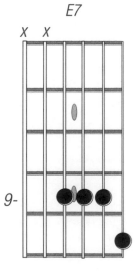

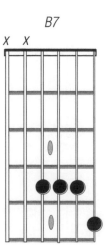

All of these chords would be switched between straight major and seventh voicings to keep things interesting. Again, I've recorded an example on the CD to give you the basic idea.

This is all well and good in the key of E, but naturally you can move these chord voicings around to other places and into other keys and still come up with something that has more of an authentic edge than the barre chords we started off considering.

So, even with these just these few new chord voicings, a blues in E can easily be transformed into something far more interesting than the norm.

Assignment

Try mixing and matching all the chord forms we've been looking at in a straightforward blues in E and explore the sound potential of all of them. You'll end up adopting something that sounds right to you – and that's the beginnings of developing your own style.

Going Further With The Dominant-Seventh Chord

Of course, we must remember here that we're still talking about accompaniment ideas here – we're not working on anything that was meant to be considered outside that framework. The guitar solo came much later on, historically speaking, although instrumentals and 'guitar rags' were quite common.

Again, it's advisable to seek out some early blues recordings and decide for yourself which elements you want to work on for your own style of playing.

So what else can this practice of switching around voicings tell us? For a start, we have to learn to recognise chord fragments – a bit like trying to spot a family resemblance. For instance – and we're beginning to come more up to date now – it's important to see this chord shape as being part of the more familiar E7:

If you compare the two versions, you'll see how we can achieve another important variation in timbre by merely missing out a few select notes here and there.

Again, it's important to see this old blues staple as being nothing more than part of the E7 chord itself:

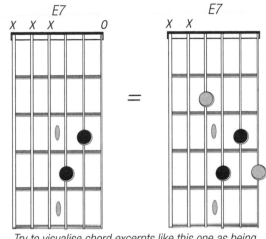

Try to visualise chord excerpts like this one as being part of a more familiar shape

Remember, one of the devices that will help you learn this sort of thing at speed is placing the information you come across within some sort of context. Knowing that the example above is a comparatively harmless E7 chord seen from a slightly different angle means that the information can be processed, stored and called upon far more reliably than it would do if it was merely 'remembered' totally devoid of context.

Another worthy dominant-seventh fragment turns up in the C shape. This shape is handy when you're not the only accompanist in the band – if you're playing with keyboards, for instance.

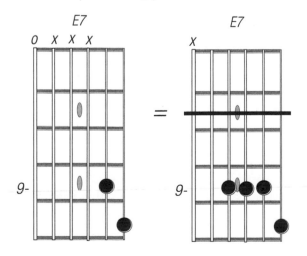

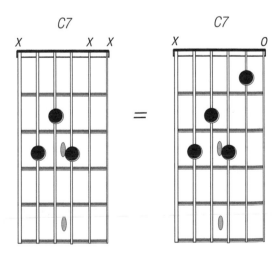

This shape is nice and subtle because it represents just the bare bones of the dominant-seventh chord. And, while we're talking about stripping down this most important of all blues chords, we might as well take a closer look at exactly what it is that constitutes a dominant seventh in the first place.

Dominant Theory And The Perfect Cuppa

Don't be put off by that word *theory* – I'm not going to put you through a college course on music. I'm just going to give you enough information for you to understand fully what a dominant seventh is and why it sounds the way it does. It'll help you to make some discoveries of your own along the way as well as improve your overall sense of music, so stick with it and I promise to be gentle.

There's an awful lot of hogwash talked about chords, scales and so on in music. It's easy to forget sometimes that all of the analysis and theorising actually came much later than the music itself did. What's more, anything that is extremely simple to do in reality looks nigh-on impossible when you start to write it down.

For instance, if I told you to write out some instructions for someone, telling them how to make the perfect cup of tea, you'd probably be surprised at how many pages of text you ended up with. You'd also notice how your own text differed from those written by others on the same subject – another parallel to music analysis!

After all, it's not just a simple case of saying, 'Put the tea in the pot, add boiling water, let it steep for a few minutes, then pour, adding milk and sugar if so desired.' Those instructions are fine as long as they're being read by someone who has made a cup of tea previously and is just going to nod in agreement, but it wouldn't suit a first-timer, would it? There's much too little information there.

For a start, there's the crucial question of exactly how much tea to use – and while we're on that subject, we might as well talk about different types of tea, where and how the plants are grown and exactly which piece of the plant is picked, subsequently dried and used in the teapot...

Then we'd have to include a few definitions: boiling water, not nearly boiling – oh, and, of course, water boils at different temperatures depending on how far you are above sea level...

And so even something as simple as teaching someone to make a cup of tea can come in for some rather grandiose analysis if we put our minds to it – and yet it's a thing that you can learn the basics of in five minutes flat if someone physically shows you the way rather than giving you a set of written instructions that you must interpret on your own. Left to experiment on your own, you'll end up making tea the way you want, just from a very basic set of principles. You'll end up, in fact, with your own tea-making style.

In a lot of instances, this is how blues was taught – by word of mouth, and certainly not written down. Like I said earlier, the analysis and all the other huffing and puffing came along when the academics and the music colleges got hold of it.

Basic Construction

So what do we need to make the perfect dominant-seventh chord? First of all, we need to know where every chord starts...

All chords come from scales. A chord is simply notes from a scale that sum up the overall sound of the scale when they're sounded together. For instance, take major chords.

```
C   D   E   F   G   A   B   C
1   2   3   4   5   6   7   1
```

Above is a C major scale, spelled out using music's standard alphabet and numbered for our convenience. If we take the first note, miss one, then take the third, miss another one and take the fifth, we end up with the following:

```
C       E       G
1       3       5
```

If you play these three particular notes together, you end up hearing the familiar sound of C major. Try it for yourself.

C maj

C E G

It sounds OK, doesn't it? Well, these three notes in these three positions have been chosen to represent every major chord in every key – and every minor chord in every minor key, too. The only difference with minor chords is that you need to start off with a minor scale – the principle is otherwise identical. So, this means that we could look at E major:

E F# G# A B C# D# E
1   2   3   4 5   6   7   1

...and take the first, third and fifth notes...

E G# B
1   3   5

...and *voilà*, an E major chord.

That's really all you need to know for now – four paragraphs – although, if you're seriously interested, I've written a book called *Chords And Scales For Guitarists* that really gives the process of making chords and scales a thorough going over – a bit like the advanced tea-making course we were looking at earlier!

OK, the shameless advert for the author's literary output is over. Now let's get back to business.

Dominant chords are a bit different from straight major and minor chords, mainly because they contain not three but four notes apiece, and they come from the dominant scale:

C D E F G A B♭ C
1 2 3 4 5 6   7   1

This scales travels under several names – the ones you're most likely to hear in these parts is either 'the dominant scale' or, slightly more frighteningly, 'the Mixolydian mode'. It's a fact that many things in music were named about three or four different times by various different societies, and just to confuse music students everywhere, the academics have decided to retain all of them. So watch out for similes in music – they're everywhere.

Vive La Différence

Like I said, a dominant chord contains four notes, the first three of which you should recognise:

C E G
1 3 ♭

It's a good, old-fashioned major chord. The fun starts when we add the seventh:

C E G B♭
1 3 5 7

If you want to hear the difference (and it's a particularly important one), take a listen to the difference between these two shapes:

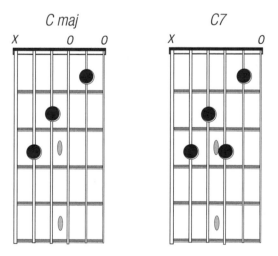

When I say listen, I mean really listen. The difference might sound quite subtle at first, but you hold in your hands one of the greatest determining factors that makes blues sound the way it does – and it's got to be in your head, too.

To make this essential difference even more pronounced, play through these two scales:

C maj scale

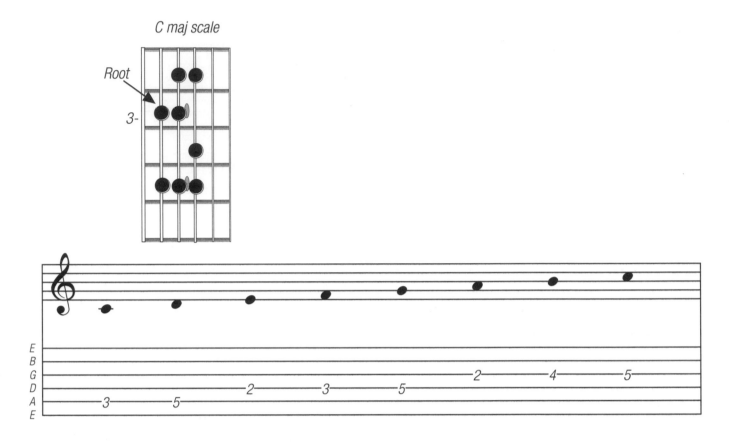

C7 scale

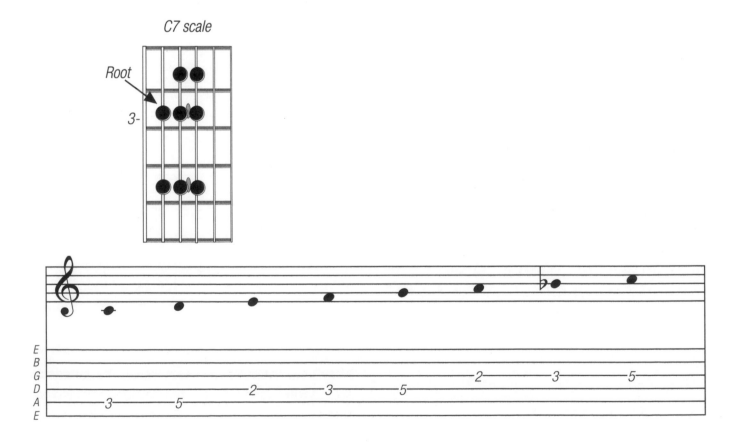

Here, the difference is even more pronounced: the dominant scale sounds as 'unfinished' and inconclusive as the chord that comes from it. Include this exercise in your practice routine until your ear can really hear the difference between the two scale identities.

The main reason why a dominant chord sounds the way it does is down to tension. In music, we talk about tension and release the same way that we would talk about day and night, ebb and flow, yin and yang – they all represent contrasting opposites. That's mainly why playing a dominant chord followed by its correct major chord sounds the way it does.

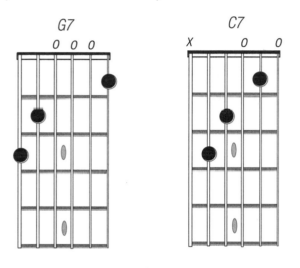

The dominant represents tension and the major chord release – or, to give both terms their more musical identities, dissonance and consonance. Naturally, the tension within the dominant chord is fairly well hidden – I mean, it doesn't sound appalling, does it? Just a little unfinished or tense. So, we have to look further inside the chord to find its inner tension – we have to look at the relationship between the notes themselves.

If you play these pairs of notes together, we'll try to hunt out the dissonant factor. First, the C and E:

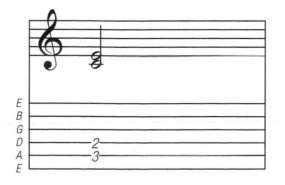

Now, the E and G:

Now the G and B♭:

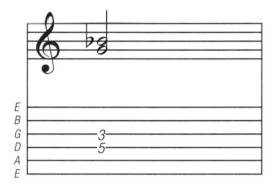

So far so good – everything sounds quite normal. But try this, the E and B♭:

Now, that's not quite so nice, is it? And there's a good reason why – and it has something to do with some of the blues's most popular folklore, so listen up!

Diabolus In Musica

The relationship between the third and seventh of any dominant-seventh chord is known as a *flat fifth*. In other words, it's a semitone (one fret) short of being a perfect fifth:

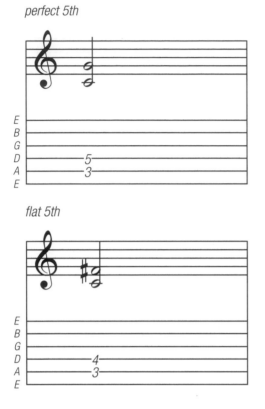

This interval, the flat fifth, gained a reputation for itself during the Middle Ages. It became known as 'the Devil's interval' for various reasons. One of the main reasons was that this particular interval sits exactly halfway along the chromatic scale:

C	C#/Db	D	D#/Eb	E	F	F#/Gb	G	G#/Ab	A	A#/Bb	B	C
1	2	3	4	5	6	7	8	9	10	11	12	1

In the chromatic scale above, it's the F#/Gb that sits midway along the scale – it's exactly the same distance from the Cs at both ends. Put simply, the churchmen of the Middle Ages thought that anything that sat exactly midway along anything had to be the work of God – but this interval sounded awful, which guaranteed it a one-way trip to Hell and it subsequently became known as the Devil's interval (look up *Diabolus In Musica* in any music dictionary). What's more, they actually banned this interval from all religious music.

So, the interval that forms the dominant-seventh chord – the principal chord in blues – has an association with the Devil. If you read about Robert Johnson earlier in this book, it might be easier to see now why blues is often referred to as being the Devil's music.

No Rest For The Wicked

If we put the dominant-to-major chord interchange under a more powerful microscope for a moment and just look at what happens to this interval in particular when the changeover happens, it's easier to see how tension becomes resolved.

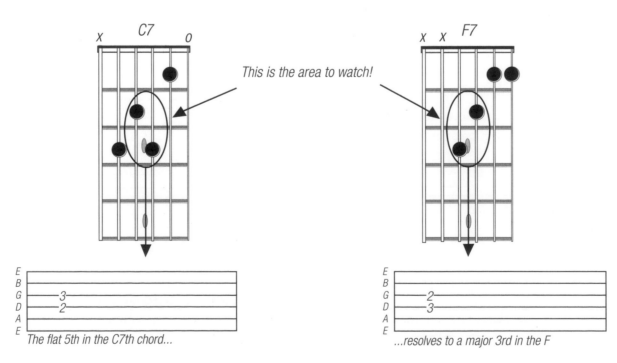

The flat 5th in the C7th chord...

...resolves to a major 3rd in the F

A lot of the strength in blues comes from keeping this interval unresolved. By linking dominant-seventh chords together – as you would do in a blues chord arrangement – this resolution hasn't a chance to happen; the music never really comes to 'rest'. Instead, you have something else altogether – more of a chord *progression*. Take a look at the two chords below:

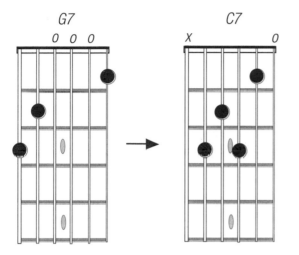

They sound like they belong together, but they don't resolve into each other as satisfactorily as this pair:

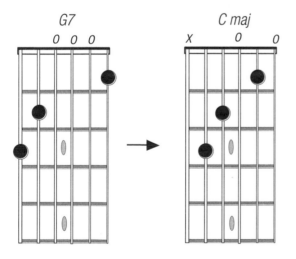

So blues harmony in general has an urgent, unresolved quality about it that suits the mood fairly well but doesn't necessarily conform to any 'book-learned' music theory.

Naturally, other types of chord crop up in blues as well; it's not uncommon to see major chords sitting

alongside their dominant counterparts every so often. The reasoning behind this is really quite simple: if you cast your mind back a few pages, you'll remember that a dominant chord starts life as a major, in any case.

$$C \text{ major} = C\ E\ G$$
$$C7 = C\ E\ G\ B\flat$$

So swapping from one to the other isn't doing anything other than offering a little variety for musician and audience alike.

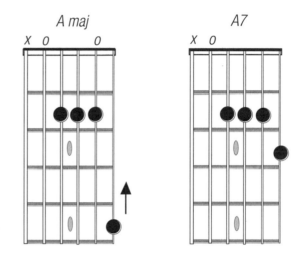

It would be true to say that you'll come across minor chords in blues, too – but not as often as you would think in a music that has the reputation for being very 'minor-sounding'.

Check out some of the Chicago blues guitar accompaniments and you'll find another type of harmony – that of *riff style*. In classical music, this form of accompaniment would be referred to as *ostinato*, which, translated back into English, means a repetitive, melodic accompaniment figure. *Riff* is very much a rock 'n' roll word, but at least we all understand it!

Much of the blues recorded during the '50s and '60s saw the guitar playing this particular role – often, I suspect, to provide a bit of counterpoint to the keyboards and generally keep the harmony moving a bit more than playing chords in a four four rhythm might have done.

Seeing as this form of blues harmony is derived from playing chord tones taken from the pentatonic scale, we'll reserve looking at it from a closer point of view until Chapter 5, 'Blues Melody'.

So it's possible to round up our initial look at blues harmony by saying that we are drawing from three essential chord types: predominantly dominant sevenths, with major and minors in arguably much lesser degrees.

So far, so good, but what about all those other types of chord that lurk around in chord books? How useful are they to a blues musician?

Other Chord Forms

If we check out the blues timeline, it really isn't until comparatively recently that other types of chord crept into the music. As we saw in the previous chapter, blues and jazz were stablemates long ago until jazz went its own way and developed its own, often entirely separate set of characteristics.

By the time blues migrated north to Chicago, there wasn't an awful lot of jazz left in it. If you like, you could say that jazz stayed in New Orleans for a while and then the beboppers took up camp in New York and an entirely different strain of music history began to be written.

Of course, this isn't to say that jazz musicians didn't play blues – they did, and there are some fine recorded examples of just how they treated it. Just look out for any compilation of saxophonist Charlie Parker's melodic treatment of a blues and you'll see how the two musics might have effectively parted company, but elements of each were retained by the other.

During the 1950s, as the song goes, blues had a baby and they called it rock 'n' roll. A predominantly 'white' music in the USA (blues was still referred to as 'race' music – and even that was a concession for people who referred to it as 'black' music) rock 'n' roll definitely stole many things from the blues – the 12-bar format cropped up quite a lot, dominant harmony wasn't at all unusual and the 'duh-duh duh-duh' accompaniment that we all know and love…

swing eighths

…was suddenly everywhere you went. Many people think that the rhythm figure above was invented alongside rock 'n' roll, but if you check out Robert Johnson's 1936 recording of 'When You Got A Good Friend', you'll find that it was already serving its time back in the Mississippi Delta long before Bill Haley was even born!

But rock 'n' roll wasn't a further development of blues itself; rather it was another form of music that sprung from it. So where do we look for the next logical step in the blues's musical history?

To begin with, the blues was taken up by a small bunch of elitists in Britain and eventually given a slightly different reading at much more intense volume levels and then re-imported back into the USA, awakening a whole generation of American people to a piece of their own home-grown culture.

But the harmonies didn't change much; the blues was in new instrumental territory, perhaps – the Chicago line-up of piano, harp, guitar, bass and drums was re-interpreted many times on these shores – but the music form itself remained pretty much intact.

Any study of '60s blues in Britain wouldn't be complete without reference to John Mayall and the rapidly changing line-up of his band, The Bluesbreakers. Virtually everything you need to know about British blues guitar is contained on the albums *John Mayall's Bluesbreakers With Eric Clapton* and the later *A Hard Road*, the latter featuring Peter Green breaking new ground on his Les Paul.

But personally, I think it was jazz that had the most pertinent interest in changing some of the blues's inner workings...

It used to be said: 'What's the difference between a jazz musician and a blues musician?' The answer is, 'A jazz musician can play blues,' implying that jazz is a more highly evolved version of blues.

It certainly seems to be true that a lot of changes seem to have happened since certain contemporary jazz players started playing blues, Robben Ford being an excellent example.

Now, it's not uncommon to find 'extended' forms of dominant-seventh chords cropping up in blues all the time – and so we ought to give them a dusting off, too.

The Jazz Influence

Don't let the word *jazz* put you off, I'm not going to lead you into any territory that isn't blues-related. It's just that extended chord forms in jazz are commonplace and it's here that we can find out how some of the 'newer' sounds have been allowed to creep into the music during the last 30 years or so.

For a start, let's define what I mean by 'extended chord forms'. So far, we've been considering three types of chord – major, minor and dominant seventh – but you'll be aware after even the most cursory look through a chord dictionary that there are plenty more fish in this particular sea, some of them being very

odd-looking little buggers you no doubt thought you'd never find a use for!

I'm talking about chords with names like these:

Cmaj9
Dmin11
E13
C9
G11
Amin7

And so on. The first job here is to assign them some sort of general identity, so here goes. As a rule, the three categories of major, minor and seventh remain, irrespective of what the chord may appear to be called. For instance, all major chords are usually have the word *major* somewhere in their titles, and so chords called...

C major 7
C major 9
C major 13
C major 6

...all belong to the major-chord family.

It's the same with minors, too. If you see a chord type with *minor* in the title, it's safe to assume that it's a member of the minor-chord fraternity.

C minor 9
C minor 7
C minor 6
C minor 7♭5

All are minor chords and can be treated as such within the context of the music you're playing.

Incidentally, we talk about whether blues is, in fact, a major or minor music and come to the conclusion (in the chapter on melody) that it's a major music with an ambiguous third – the note from the scale that determines major or minor in Western music.

In fact, actually minor blues are very uncommon, although, naturally, they do exist. In such cases, the I and IV chords are both minor, but the V chord is still a dominant, as normal. Out in the field, you are more likely to find a blues 'hybrid' which is bluesy in nature, with minor chords in it, but leaning more towards 'rock' harmony. A perfect example of this would be Led Zeppelin's 'Since I've Been Loving You', which has all the qualities of a blues but contains mainly minor chords and breaks away from the straightforward 12-bar format, adhering more to song form, complete with a chorus.

Dominant Chords (Slight Return)

When we get to dominant chords – and remember that we're talking about the predominant type of chord found in blues – we seem to have the largest choice available:

$$C7$$
$$C9$$
$$C11$$
$$C13$$
$$C7\flat9$$
$$C7\sharp9$$
$$C7\sharp5$$

These are all dominant types of chord and, like the other two families, can be treated similarly.

I find it's useful to think of the three family groups as being like colours and the different types of chord found within their groups being the different tones of those colours. We'd all agree that there is more than one colour red, wouldn't we? There's light red, blood red, scarlet, and so on. So it is with chord variations. Let's see exactly why this is.

We've seen that dominant-seventh chords are made up from four basic notes...

$$C \quad E \quad G \quad B\flat$$
$$1 \quad 3 \quad 5 \quad 7$$

...and that they spring from the dominant scale:

$$C \quad D \quad E \quad F \quad G \quad A \quad B\flat \quad C$$
$$1 \quad 2 \quad 3 \quad 4 \quad 5 \quad 6 \quad 7 \quad 1$$

So what happens when we add more notes from the scale to the basic seventh? For instance, we could add the note D to a C dominant chord:

$$C \quad E \quad G \quad B\flat \quad D$$
$$1 \quad 3 \quad 5 \quad 7 \quad 9$$

You'll notice immediately that the D – the second note of the scale – has been renamed the *ninth*. This is a music convention that insists we consider two octaves for the naming of chords, so that things look like this:

$$C \quad D \quad E \quad F \quad G \quad A \quad B\flat \quad C \quad D \quad E \quad F \quad G \quad A \quad B\flat \quad C$$
$$1 \quad 2 \quad 3 \quad 4 \quad 5 \quad 6 \quad 7 \quad 1 \quad 9 \quad 3 \quad 11 \quad 5 \quad 13 \quad 7 \quad 1$$

So, the D has to be called the ninth to indicate that the seventh is in the chord somewhere, too. Now, don't worry about this – I don't want to complicate your life by spending the next page or so telling you the reasoning behind the naming of chords; we are, after all, trying to keep things as simple as possible.

If, however, you're the type of person who just HAS TO KNOW the answer to these types of riddle, then there's always that other book of mine I shamelessly plugged a few pages ago. It's all in there...

The most important thing here is to acknowledge that a C7 and a C9 are basically different shades of the same basic colour. (You could think of them as being different flavours, if you prefer.)

Listen to both of them:

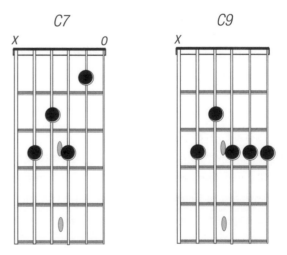

Instead of trying to hear how different they are, I want you to try to hear their similarities. They both have the all-important stem of notes in them:

$$C7 = 1 \ 3 \ 5 \ 7$$
$$C9 = 1 \ 3 \ 5 \ 7 \ 9$$

The extra note is just there for the sake of adding 'colour'. Try this test: play through this blues once using C7, and then again using C9 instead:

First:

‖ C7 / / /| C7 / / /| C7 / / /| C7 / / / |
| F7 / / /| F7 / / /| C7 / / /| C7 / / / |
| G7 / / /| F7 / / /| C7 / / /| C7 / / / ‖

Then:

‖ C9 / / /| C9 / / /| C9 / / /| C9 / / / |
| F7 / / /| F7 / / /| C9 / / /| C9 / / / |
| G7 / / /| F7 / / /| C9 / / /| C9 / / / ‖

You should be able to hear what I mean about C9 representing a different 'shade' of C7 straight away. Now, try this:

‖ C7 / / /| C9 / / /| C7 / / /| C9 / / / |
| F7 / / /| F7 / / /| C7 / / /| C9 / / / |
| G7 / / /| F7 / / /| C7 / / /| C9 / / / ‖

You can hear how there's a variation there when you play the C chord, and it's not something that's changing the basic function of the chord, merely its hue.

This is what jazz started to do to blues. The introduction of more colourful chords made the harmony sound more vibrant. You can hear how, once the ear has been distracted away from the dominant-seventh sound, the music takes on a different nature. The relentless 'dom 7' accompaniment gives the blues a lot of its essential characteristic: it's meant to be repetitive; it's not meant to stray too far from the original harmony if it's to remain 'pure' and Delta-bound.

When we do vary the harmony, a lot gets taken away from the purity of the original music form, but it opens the gate for other interesting things to happen.

Assignment

Hunt out chord shapes for the following chords and see how they would fit inside a C blues:

C9
C13
C11
C7♭5
C7♯9
C7♭9

Some of the chord forms above will work straight away, while others won't stand too much repetition, but even they have a space inside the blues framework.

Extended Dominant Chords

'I like altered chords, I like using them. Flat-five chords, raised-ninth chords, 13ths and so on. They add a lot of character to a blues.' *Robben Ford*

You'll have noticed in the assignment above that there are chords with '♯9' and other similar instructions attached to them. What's all this about?

Well, given that all the notes we can add to a basic C7 are drawn from two octaves of its scale...

C	D	E	F	G	A	B♭	C	D	E	F	G	A	B♭	C
1	2	3	4	5	6	7	1	9	3	11	5	13	7	1

...what happens when we've used all of them? The answer is that we look to the chromatic scale for more notes to add! So...

C	C♯/D♭	D	D♯/E♭	E	F	F♯/G♭	G	G♯/A♭	A	A♯/B♭	B	C
1	2	3	4	5	6	7	8	9	10	11	12	1

I make it five other notes that we could add to the basic dominant-seventh stem to produce yet more variations in chord colour. If you want the maths...

- 7 notes in the basic dominant scale
- 12 notes in the chromatic scale
- 12 − 7 = 5

These notes are would be as follows:

C♯/D♭	D♯/E♭	F♯/G♭	G♯/A♭	B
1	2	3	4	5

When superimposed on top of the dominant scale, they are given new names to specify their positions within the scale:

C#/Db	D#/Eb	F#/Gb	G#/Ab	B
b9	#9	b5	#5	♮7

So that's where we get chord names like 'C7#9' from. Its formula would read thus:

$$C7\sharp9 = C \ E \ G \ B\flat \ D\sharp$$
$$1 \ 3 \ 5 \ 7 \ \sharp9$$

So you can see that the all-important C7 stem is still perfectly intact, it's just that we've got a new colour tone to play with:

C7♯9

Any chord book will be able to direct you towards the vast number of extended dominants available. Most of them, it has to be said, fall well beyond the scope of blues and head off into jazz territory.

Jazz is a very chromatically enhanced music — it depends on push and pull between consonance and dissonance. Blues is much more simple, from both harmonic and melodic points of view, and so it can get by via a much simpler set of fundamentals.

'Jazz is just blues with more difficult chords in it...'
Martin Taylor

In the next chapter, which concentrates on blues melody, we'll see that an understanding of how the blues turns up in jazz is actually easier to appreciate from the point of view of studying jazz and not the other way around.

It's actually quite unlikely that you'll find too many extended chords in your day-to-day blues playing. Even the most modern blues tends to rely very much on the examples set for it nearly 100 years ago — which means that, as far as this particular timeline is concerned, we've come up to date.

5 BLUES MELODY

'There are times when somebody like BB or Eric, when they play, look round at me and say, "Come on, play!"
and I say, "Look man, you play, I'll listen. I'm trying to learn something!"' Buddy Guy

There's little doubt that the melodic tradition in the blues started with unaccompanied voice. The original field hollers and work songs were without instrumental backing – that came later on. There were a few more layers of musical strata to be formed before we ended up with anything like we know today as instrumental blues.

When the guitar began to take its place as the principal blues instrument, it was the inflections of the singing voice that it tried to imitate. In fact, it has been said that the origins of slide guitar were down to the fact that a slide could imitate the 'wailing' nature of the original blues hollers, or early melodies, far more accurately. Certainly, the idea of bending strings and that distinctive blues vibrato originated with vocal inflections.

For years, the guitar was seen as being primarily an accompanying instrument – the days of the guitar solo as we know it were a long way off. Originally, if a guitar played 'solo', it meant an unaccompanied solo instrumental piece – like a guitar rag, for instance. The only purely melodic information contained in the early blues pieces were in the forms of intros, turnarounds and endings – plus the odd descriptive sound effect like Robert Johnson's 'howling wind' on 'Come On In My Kitchen'.

So how did the guitar solo develop from simple accompaniment? Well, for a start, melody and harmony have such close links with one another that it's not a particularly hard job to see how one gave life to the other. But there are a couple of things that we have to consider first.

The African Influence

You can't really talk about blues melody in any great detail without looking way back to the dark times of the slave trade and the systematic and barbaric relocation of men, women and children from the west coast of Africa to the cotton fields of America's Deep South. Attempts were made to rid these unwilling immigrants of their cultural heritage by splitting up families and tribes, forbidding the use of their own language, banning any musical instrument that was thought in any way to be 'tribal' in origin and by various other means, too.

But no one can strip such a rich cultural – and musical – heritage away completely, and inevitably much of it remained to surface as an influence on incoming Western musical traditions.

Now, if you read the chapter on blues history, you'll remember that I said that I won't try to turn you into an ethnomusicologist, because that's not what we're here for. I believe it's good for any musician to gain knowledge about the origins of his chosen musical style, but we needn't involve ourselves here with anything more than a thumbnail sketch. If you're fascinated, as I was, about the origins of blues, there are many books out there that will fill in the blanks in much more detail than I can here. We'll just concern ourselves with the beginnings of blues melody and leave it at that.

It's been said before that blues was born from the clash between cultures – east meets west, as simple as that. It's more complex than that, of course, but that idea will serve us for now.

If you can picture what might have happened if a person from a strictly West African musical culture attempted to rationalise songs that must have sounded wrong to his ears, then you've got the starting place for the melodic 'compromise' that was to give birth to some of the anomalies we meet when talking about the blues scale as a musical exercise.

Major Or Minor?

To begin with, is blues minor or major in character? It's a difficult one to call, because we're talking about seemingly minor scales being in place over basically major chords. Take a look at a breakdown of a dominant-seventh chord and the minor pentatonic scale (the predominant scale for use in blues melody or guitar solos):

$C7 = C\ E\ G\ B\flat$
     1 3 5 7

C minor pentatonic = C E♭ F G B♭ C

Doesn't really work, does it? And the reason why it doesn't is all to do with the E♭ in the scale clashing with the E in the chord. If you were to play these two notes together on the fretboard, you'd get this effect:

You can see immediately that this just doesn't work – and the reason for this is that, as far as blues is concerned, they are both wrong.

The definition between major and minor thirds – which is, musically speaking, what we're dealing with here – is all very well for most forms of Western music,

including classical music and a lot of popular music, but when it comes down to blues, the third sound we're looking for actually lies somewhere in between the two.

You can test this out for yourself. Below are two examples. The first is a major third, the second a minor third:

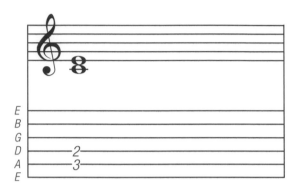

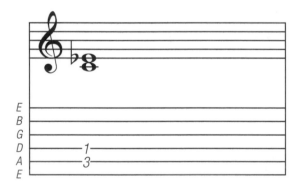

Imagine trying to fit either of these into a blues context. It doesn't quite go the whole distance, does it? Now try this:

Bend this note slightly sharp

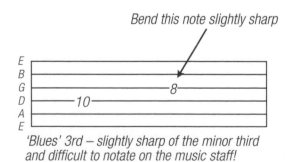

'Blues' 3rd – slightly sharp of the minor third and difficult to notate on the music staff!

What we have here is a musical pitch that lies somewhere in between major and minor; it shouldn't actually exist and there is not even a formal way of writing it down in standard notation (we could refer to it as the ±3rd, I guess, but that's probably too mathematical – I prefer calling it the 'blue third'). But it sounds right. It sounds bluesy.

The reasoning behind this is embedded deep in that clash of musical cultures we've been talking about. An interval that exists quite happily in the tribal music of the African west coast, and one that has been ingrained in the musical consciousness of the people there to such an extent that Western musical practices couldn't purge it, caused one of the foremost sounds of the blues: the blue third.

And this is how this particular scale is played 90 per cent of the time in a blues or blues-influenced context. It probably represents the largest step in terms of turning a purely Western musical idea into something that fits the hybrid nature of the blues.

Harmony And Melody

Just a few more words of explanation and, I hope, clarification, before I begin to sketch out blues melody on the fretboard for you. I'm really trying to keep theory to an absolute minimum here because I'm aware that actual theory isn't going to be of much use to you if all you're aiming to do is play a perfect rendition of 'Sweet Home Chicago' at the drop of a hat!

I just want to draw you one more picture – of how harmony and melody are interrelated from the start in music. To begin with, both are made from the exact

Right, we've established one of the principal anomalies of the blues, but let's take a step back to this major/minor interface and see what exactly happens if we allow for the third to be neither one or the other:

C7 = C E G B♭
    1 3 5 7

C minor pentatonic = C E/E♭ F G B♭ C

We've got more of a perfect fit than before, that's for sure. So, if I were to rewrite the minor pentatonic scale to allow for the blue third, it would begin to look like this:

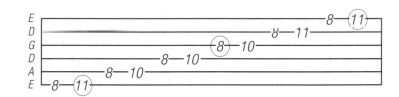

Bend circled notes slightly sharp

same materials; if I were to write out the common chords in the key of C major that are drawn upon to accompany folk tunes and so on, you'd see that they are directly related to the scale of C major:

Cmaj = C E G
Fmaj = F A C
G7 = G B D F

Lay all the notes contained in these chords end to end and we have this:

C E G F A C G B D F

Put them in alphabetical order, starting on C:

C D E F F G G A B C

Lose the notes that are repeated:

C D E F G A B C

And we're back to the scale. So, both chords and scales are made from exactly the same materials – that's their basic relationship or interdependence summed up. The very basic (and here, very approximate, too!) method for harmonising a melody in C major is based on the fact that some melody notes (ie scale tones) will be supported by the C chord, some by the F and some by the G7. From this, you can see that the relationship is a tight one – even symbiotic, one might say.

So how do we apply all this to the blues? Let's do exactly the same trick with the basic minor pentatonic with a blue third and see if it works.

C7 = C E G B♭

      1 3 5 7

C minor pentatonic = C E/E♭ F G B♭ C

You can see straight away that the scale is practically all chord tones, for a start! So it's no wonder that even the most hit-or-miss attempts at soloing using this scale will sound semi-successful – you can't play a wrong note if all you're playing are notes that are already in the chord, after all.

A solo made up from random pentatonic scale tones might not sound like the greatest piece of music ever written, but it's not going to sound bad – maybe just a tad directionless, that's all.

Of course, the odd man out in terms of pentatonic chord tones is the F; and you might have found that there is a sort of grey area within the scale where everything stops working for a moment or two. This usually means that you've discovered the F.

Does this mean that the blues scale is actually only five notes long, though? After all, we've been talking about only a basic pentatonic scale so far. Most Western musical scales are seven notes long, and so is blues the real maverick that we think it is?

Here, we need a bit more context. It'll take only a paragraph, so bear with me...

It's a fact that most music cultures across the world can own up to having at least one pentatonic scale to their name. It seems that all 'folk' music – that is, music that is usually handed down in a purely aural tradition and not 'book-learnt' or 'composed' – shares the five-note scale idea, whether it be in Japan, Africa, Europe, or wherever.

Blues is definitely a folk music – or, at least, it was originally. It even corresponds from a lyrical point of view in that a lot of early blues were just stories set to music, and often autobiographical at that. Similarly, a lot of early folk music in Britain were true stories of love lost, tragic losses, and so on.

So, back in the early days, it would certainly have been true to say that a lot of blues was purely pentatonic – but more and more has been added to it along the way. In other words, blues evolved along its timeline, and in the process, certain of its traditions were modified to suit.

The Blues Scale

If we take the basic pentatonic scale, with added blue third, it would look like this:

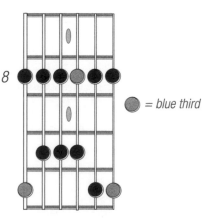

Notice that the blue thirds are still defined as being in a single place – this is to make what we're going to do now a little easier to understand. It's to be taken for granted that these pitches shown here must all be bent slightly sharp.

One other important addition to the scale – and one that really brings out its bluesy qualities more fully – is the flat fifth. If you remember, the flat fifth was referred to as 'the Devil's interval' in ages past and so it really is appropriate that it should turn up in blues, I suppose.

The flat fifth sits here in this particular shape:

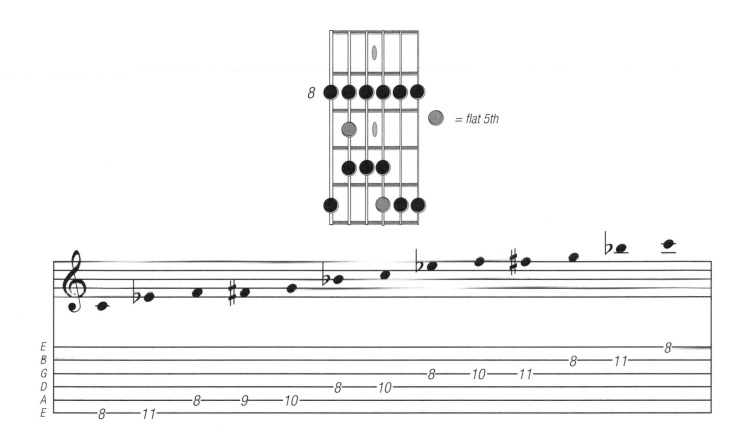

Play the scale through and listen to how it sounds with this new member on board. The effect it has – apart from adding yet another healthy dose of blues to the scale – is to smoothe out these two areas:

So, if we write out this new version of the scale, what are we left with now?

C blues scale = C E♭/E F G♭ G B♭ C

This is probably as close as we can get for now. I wouldn't like to stick my neck out and say which exact era of the blues's development we've reached – in other words I'm not going to make any grand pronouncements like, 'This takes us up to 1937,' or anything like that. I will say, however, that I think we're still pretty crude, in terms of what is in use today.

We'll add some more notes to what we've got already in a while, but for now let's make sure we're taking advantage of what we've got already.

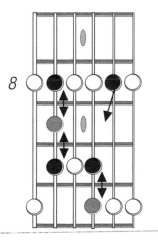

The flat 5th 'smoothes out' the transition between scale tones in these areas

Learning Scales

It's always at this point that I turn apologetic: yes, learning scales is absolutely vital if you're thinking along the lines of being able to play guitar solos with confidence. If blues is your thing, then making sure that you know all the variations of the pentatonic minor scale all over the neck is a pretty good place to start.

You'd be amazed at how many seminars I've given where I've ask a collection of students – some of whom have ticked the Advanced box on the booking form – if they're familiar with the pentatonic scale in all positions. Usually, at this point the room goes very quiet! They're familiar with the pentatonic scale, but only in two positions, and sometimes only one – and this simply isn't enough.

In order to play the music with real confidence and put literally every means at your disposal, you need to know the pentatonic scale thoroughly in all five positions. There really is no getting around the fact that you have to learn them. I've been asked all sorts of squirmingly embarrassed and defensive questions in the past, such as, 'Does Eric Clapton/Jimi Hendrix/Stevie Ray Vaughan know it in all five, then?' The answer is yes. Eric, Jimi or Stevie couldn't play half of what they have played on record knowing only one or two – and I'm going to prove it to you during the rest of this chapter.

At the end of this book, you'll find a fairly comprehensive scale section, giving you something to practise from, but for now we'll look at how the scale spreads itself over the fretboard in a way that's fairly easy to memorise.

Completing The Picture

I think it's probably quite safe to say that this particular position is already familiar to you:

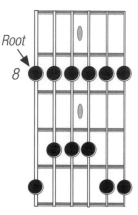

If not, it's a good place to start, as it falls under the fingers quite nicely. The way to practise it is shown in the tab here:

You'll notice that we're playing the scale from root to root each time – in this case, from C to C. This is vital, because scales shouldn't just exist in your mind as shapes on the fretboard; they should be sounds in your head, too. To sum up: scales should be in both the head and the hands.

It's no good just knowing the shape; music isn't like a kit of individual parts that just fits together somehow. In fact, what happens is that the music starts in your head, which then gives instructions to the

hands, and so it's the exact opposite of many of the hit-or-miss ('shouting and pointing') attempts I've heard at seminars.

So always play any scale from root to root so that you're hearing it in its correct context and not just a random series of notes. As we shall see, scale tones are not all equal; there's a hierarchy involved here.

So, we've dealt with the most familiar shape; what's next on the agenda? How about the shapes that go either side?

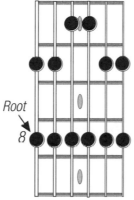

This one attaches itself to the left hand side of the first scale shape, and once again the tab shows you how to play it from root to root.

The next shape we're going to look at proceeds up the neck on the right-hand side of the one that we started with.

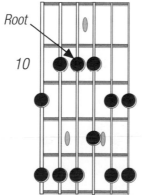

Follow the tab on this one, too. Although it might look like you're starting halfway through, you've got to play it in such a way that it gets the musical information inside your head in the right order.

There are only two left to complete the circle. Try this one first:

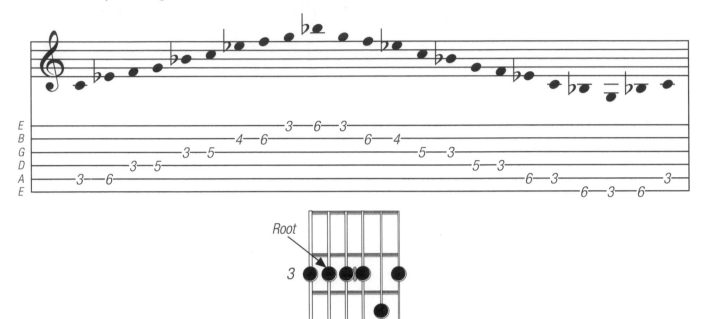

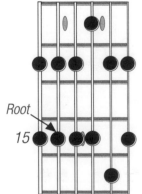

Finally, there's this shape to learn. Practise it slowly to get to grips with it.

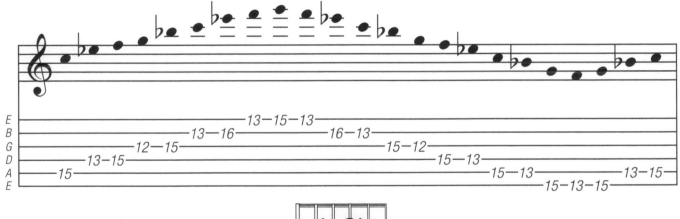

To prove that you've now covered the entire fretboard in this one particular scale shape, take a look at this:

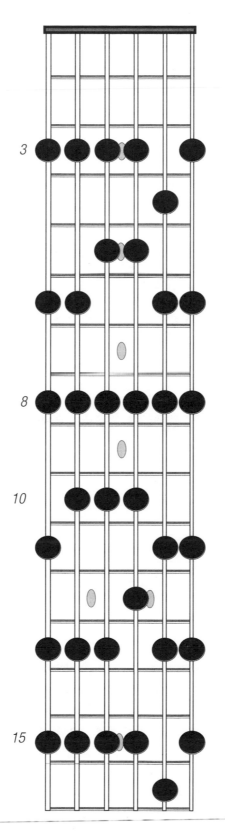

The entire fretboard covered with the five C minor pentatonic shapes

After you've completed all of these five scale shapes, all that happens is that the same shapes begin to repeat further up the fretboard. This is shown in the following diagram:

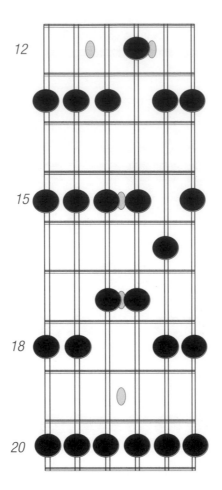

The pentatonic shapes start to repeat themselves further up the neck...

Now, I'll say again that your first task is to learn all of these shapes by heart – in fact, you've really got to know them in your sleep. You ought to be able to hum a pentatonic scale, too. If you can't, the music isn't yet established enough in your head and you need to work some more to get it there!

Mapping Out The Fretboard

The pentatonic minor scale is so important as a basic template for playing blues lines that you need to be familiar with it in all keys. This might sound like a mammoth amount of work to undertake, but if you think about it, it's not. The reasons for this are:

- You're talking about a static series of shapes which are always in the same order in every key. Learn it thoroughly once and all you've got to be able to do is relocate it according to key.

- loads of other guitarists have already done this groundwork, most of them with full marks!

In order to prove the point about the same shapes repeating the same order each time, take a look at these next diagrams – two blues keys, two fretboards with the pentatonic all over it, the same shapes, same order each time.

A minor

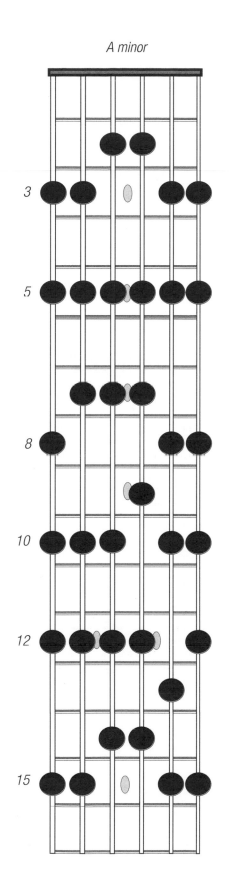

E minor

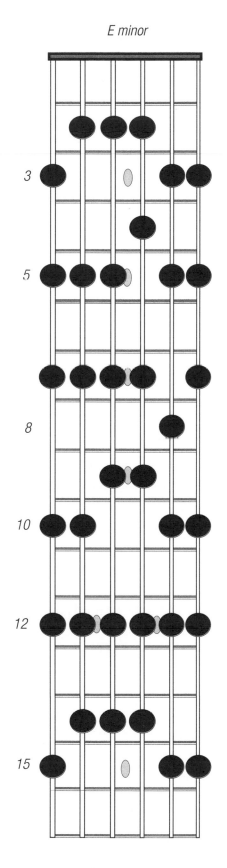

There's a rather more comprehensive guide to the pentatonic scales in the important keys in the back of this book. Use it to learn from, by all means, but remember that it's absolutely vital to commit these things to memory. Imagine you're in the army: it's like assembling an AK47 blindfold – if you can't do it by touch and feel alone, you're no good to anyone out there in the field!

Finding Pentatonic Scales In Different Keys

Once you're reasonably sure-footed, as far as putting all the pentatonic scales together *en masse* along the fretboard is concerned, the next thing to do is to move the overall pattern around to different keys. Don't, whatever you do, practise the scales over and over in one key, because that will have the effect of locking you in to one particular key and all the others will feel strange and 'out of position'.

I've seen this snag crop up with guitar students so often, and it's actually a really easy pitfall to avoid. All you need to do is keep things moving so that the hand and eye don't have a chance to lock on to a single key; you need to bring things about so that each key feels like merely a single, repetitive pattern. This state of mind guarantees you complete freedom on the fretboard – there will be no difference between playing a blues in C major or G♭. It will all feel immediately natural.

So how do we go about practising this particular area? The best plan is to learn how to locate the scales in different keys – and, before you dismiss this as being an impossible trick to pull off, let me say this: it's no more difficult than learning to move a few major barre chords around, OK?

The first thing you're going to need is a chart of the neck with all the notes written out on it. I'd advise you to miss out all of the flats and sharps at first, though, as this tends to make things look far too crowded and confusing on the neck.

The reason why I advise you to write a chart out for yourself is all down to what we in the business call *pen memory*. You may remember at school being asked to write out a poem or a section from a play in order to help you learn it. The reasons for writing out a neck chart are the same: writing it down simply focuses your attention on the individual notes and positions. Trust me – you'll be surprised how much this can help you find your way around the fretboard more quickly.

In order to help out, I'm going to include a chart here for reference, but I would still counsel you to write out your own, because yours needs to be bigger than any I can reproduce here.

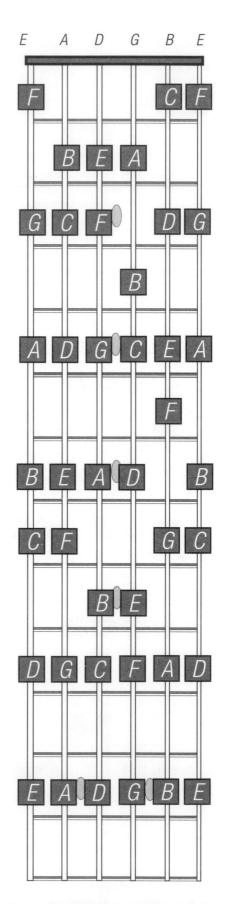

A neck chart, showing the position of the 'whole notes' only. Yours needs to be bigger than this though!

If you study this chart carefully, you should be able to see that it's not really a problem to find the sharps and flats. Take a closer look at this particular area of the fretboard:

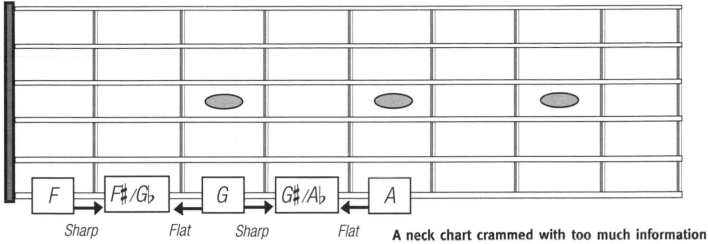

Sharp   *Flat*   *Sharp*   *Flat*

A neck chart crammed with too much information will serve only to confuse matters. Keep it simple and leave off the sharps and flats

This note is G on the third fret, bass string. The note G♯ will be positioned one fret to the right – that's the fourth fret – and G♭ will be one fret to the left, on the second. I believe it's better to know this than to have a chart that's crammed full of notes – remember, you'd not only have to write out G♯, you'd have to put A♭ in the same place, and so things would start to look way too busy.

Keep your neck chart with you – in your guitar case or pinned to a wall. It needs to be in sight when you do scale-location work so that it drip-feeds its information into your psyche over a period of time.

Now you need to know how to locate all the scale shapes. We do this by looking for *root notes*. If this shape is a major chord...

...and this note is a C...

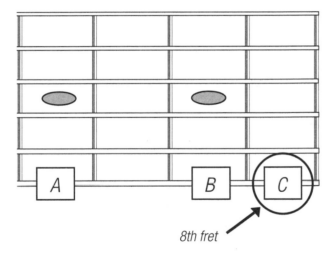

8th fret

...putting them together makes a C major barre chord:

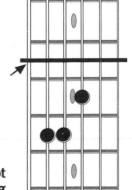

E-shape barre chord with its root on the sixth string

8

QED, as they say in the Maths department. It's exactly the same job where scales are concerned: all you need to know is the location of the root notes and you're away. So, here is the infamous 'first position' pentatonic scale with its root notes on display:

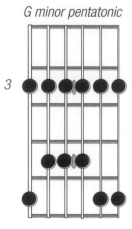

G minor pentatonic

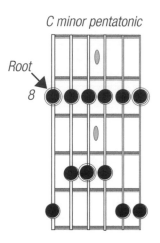

C minor pentatonic

All you have to do is line the root notes up on your chart and you can quite easily move the scale around to any key you like. Get the idea? Now all you need is the other shapes with their root notes marked and you've got the complete picture.

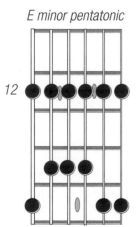

E minor pentatonic

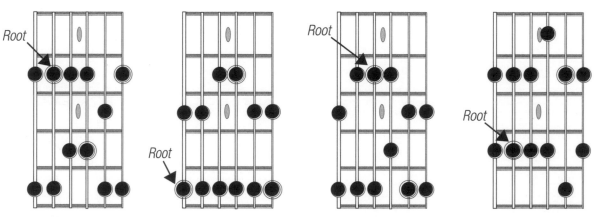

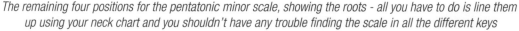

The remaining four positions for the pentatonic minor scale, showing the roots - all you have to do is line them up using your neck chart and you shouldn't have any trouble finding the scale in all the different keys

Practice tip: in accordance with the advice above about not getting stuck in a single key, pick a new key every day at random (I get my pupils to close their eyes and point to the neck chart to make the choice). Then, all you have to do is play through a couple of scales in that key and move on. This way around, keeping yourself 'fresh' in the scale area takes only a couple of minutes and doesn't have the chance to become laborious.

Advanced Minor Pentatonic Theory

'What Johnny Guitar Watson was doing was not just pentatonic scales. One of things I admired was his tone – this wiry, nasty, aggressive and penetrating tone – and another was the fact that the things that he would play would often come out as rhythmic outbursts over the constant beat of the accompaniment.' *Frank Zappa*

Anything with 'advanced' in the title is going to sound important, but what I mean here is, if you try to rush ahead into this next section, without digging the trenches as advised in the last, it's not going to make a whole lot of sense to you. So, in the spirit of 'one more time', please make sure you know all five positions of the minor pentatonic before proceeding any further with your studies. Imagine that this is a car maintenance manual – miss a bit and you'll have a lot of parts left over and the engine won't work!

The reason why these two sections carry such a vital order to them is this: learning the five positions is a hard slog – I know, because I've been there myself and, as a teacher, I've put many other people through the same kind of basic training. Now we've reached a point where I can show you a couple of shortcuts that will help to unravel some of those licks you've been trying to dig out from your CD collection recently.

Now, it might not necessarily come as a shock to you to learn that, while guitarists as a breed aren't exactly prone to being lazy, they do tend to enjoy the benefits of an easy life. What's more, you may have noticed that in many cases, at least, the five pentatonic positions repeat themselves a lot. For instance, these notes here...

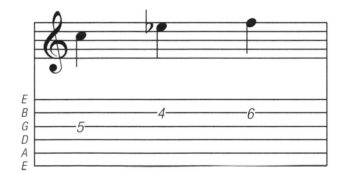

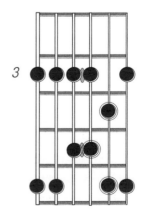

...are merely these notes here, in a different place on the fretboard:

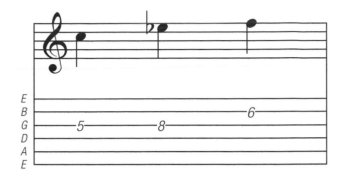

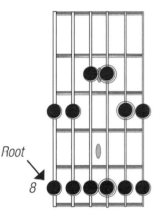

Root

So surely this strengthens the case for not having to know all positions on the fretboard, doesn't it? No! They're the same notes, no doubt about that, but they're easier to play in the first example than they are in the second, certainly where some familiar licks are concerned.

Each position of the pentatonic scale has a bevy or riffs and licks attached to it, and if you miss one out, you're not going to be able to play a handful of licks properly because you won't know where to find them. (I put this in because, human nature being what it is, many of you will have skipped the warnings about not being properly prepared for this section until you've completed the former and are now sneaking a look. I know who you are! Go back and do the job properly!)

Where were we? Oh yes. Guitarists invariably opt for the path of least resistance – and this includes fingering scales. You'll have found, no doubt, that some parts of the scales are easier to finger than others. For instance, this bit of the scale would be fingered using fingers 1 and 3:

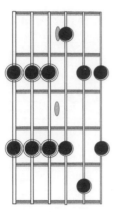

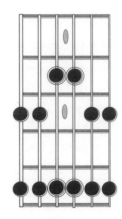

The circled section of this scale shape is very handy for a '1–3' fingering as it literally falls under the fingers...

...but these notes would represent quite a stretch for fingers 1 and 3

But this little excerpt shown above (known colloquially as the 'Layla configuration' – I'll leave you to work out exactly why!) is a bit of a stretch for fingers 1 and 3. And there's that question of agility with finger 4 – can it really cut the mustard? Is it too short? Will we be able to add vibrato to the note here – or can we even bend it?

Of course, all of these questions have been answered in the past, and this has resulted in a certain

fingering becoming established for the scales, which means that you're using only fingers 1 and 3 all the time. But – and here's the really clever bit – it's a fingering that uses all of the scale positions and not just one.

If you're currently muttering something along the lines of, 'So that's why we need to know all the positions, then?', you're bang on target. Take a quick look at this:

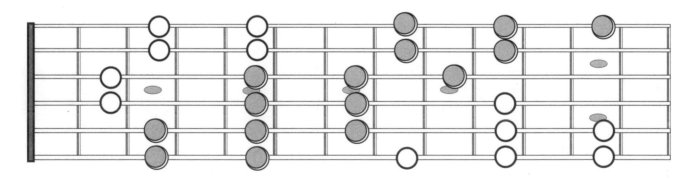

 = horizontal pentatonic scale position

The 'horizontal' pentatonic scale in A minor. The white scale tones are shown for reference

Here's a scale that moves between the third fret, bass string, right up to the top string, 12th fret – and it uses a single fingering system. Moving between the various positions, using slides to relocate between each, we've got a good, uniform scale network that now makes you look at the fretboard from a different point of view – horizontally instead of just vertically, if you like.

'I like the way the note A sounds on the top string much better than I do on the second, though I like A on the second string better than I do on the third, and so on. So, if I want to play a melody, I think of it as running along the strings rather than across them, to take advantage of that. If there is any way to do it that way, then I will do it.' *Pat Metheny*

Armed with this information, you've got not only a good way of getting between all the pentatonic positions, you've got a uniform fingering regime built into it. And you know what? There's only two of these 'horizontal' pentatonic shapes to learn. Here's the other one:

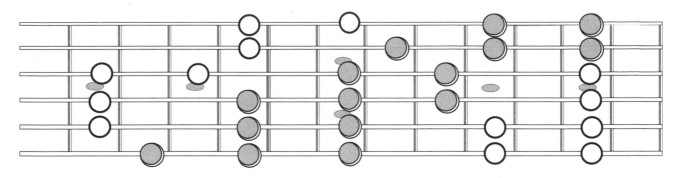

 = horizontal pentatonic scale position

The second 'horizontal' pentatonic scale in A minor. Once again, the white scale tones are there for visual reference (notice how positions 1 and 2 coincide at certain points)

Get the idea? Just two scale shapes cover the whole neck with a practical version of the pentatonic scale – and these are the ones you've been listening to on records for ages. Certainly anything that comes from the 1960s or thereabouts would have used this scale system, which makes it a very good one to include in your own scale armoury. My own 'research' in this area has revealed that Clapton employed the second of the horizontal pentatonic configurations extensively during his tenures with The Bluesbreakers and The Cream.

Naturally, now you know this particular system, you'll want the facility to move it around, as we have been doing with the five 'vertical' shapes we began looking at a while ago. So, with this in mind, here are both scale shapes with their root notes clearly marked:

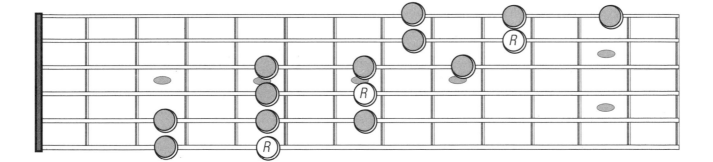

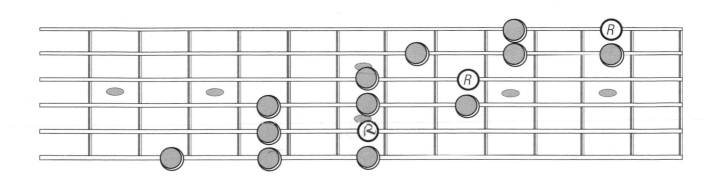

After noting this, the practice routine is very similar to before: pick a different key at random each day and work out where the two scale shapes lie on the fretboard. If you have done all this work in the correct sequence, you'll actually find this task quite easy, because the guitar neck isn't going to look as scary as it did when you started shifting things around in the first place.

Always remember that this kind of work will take time to complete, and so don't be tempted to rush any particular stage out of frustration, boredom or lack of patience. If things are done slowly, methodically and in the correct sequence, I can practically guarantee you results, given time. If you rush things, however, you won't give yourself the chance to learn any one particular stage thoroughly enough and the confusion will remain! Be thorough, methodical and patient.

Moving Forward

I guess that, if we refer to our timeline of blues development, the minor pentatonic, with its 'genderless' third – that is, the third of the scale being neither wholly major nor minor but somewhere in between – carries us forward over quite a reasonable amount of time and territory.

If you listen to blues from the early part of the last century, you'll find that this scale practically predominated, as far as blues melody is concerned. And remember, we're talking about actual vocal melody here rather than the guitar solos that were to come into fashion much later on.

So we've really done a great deal of groundwork to establish the sound of early blues at a comparatively early point in our own development as blues musicians.

If you've completed the work I've set for you so far, then the minor version of the pentatonic scale will surely hold no fear for you in the slightest. You'll be familiar with it in most keys and well aware of the way it disagrees with Western musical thinking by way of its ambiguous third note and tendency towards inviting the flat fifth into the whole process as an occasional visitor.

Here's the fretboard diagram:

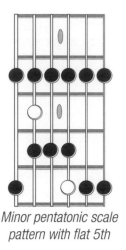

Minor pentatonic scale pattern with flat 5th

So where do we go next? The melodic story isn't yet fully told – you may feel that there is definitely still some melodic information missing from what we already know and are eager to track it down.

As blues expanded its musical brief and became wider in its influences, certain things began to happen to it in a melodic sense. We're talking about a period when it was possible to hear the blues – and other popular music – on record and radio, and so the great melting pot of influences upon the music received another stir and bits of jazz and early soul managed to creep in, broadening the blues database still further.

To my ears, listening back to some of the historic recordings of the time, what happened was that blues became even more of a major-scale music than it had been before. It still kept its minor qualities via the schizophrenic qualities of the third – this was an important factor in maintaining the yearning, wailing quality of the music in general – but there was something else in there, too.

By the time blues reached Chicago, guitarists of the time were already putting in some accompaniment ideas that would later become expanded by horn sections (see the 'Accompaniment Ideas' section in the Appendix), and a lot of these were drawn from chords like major sixths and dominant ninths. Neither the sixth nor ninth appears naturally in the minor pentatonic scale, so the music was expanded melodically to accept these new tones.

Let's have a look at what's happening here, taking the following accompaniment idea as an example of new ideas that were beginning to filter through.

Look at the chords opposite. The shape on the left is a fragment of a major sixth, made up like this:

Cmajor6 = C E G A
         1 3 5 6

Chord fragment = C E A
           1 3 6

The shape on the right is a fragment of a ninth:

C9 = C E G B♭ D
    1 3 5 7 9

Chord fragment = B♭ D G
           7 9 5

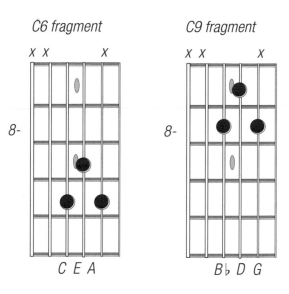

C6 fragment   *C9 fragment*

C E A   *B♭ D G*

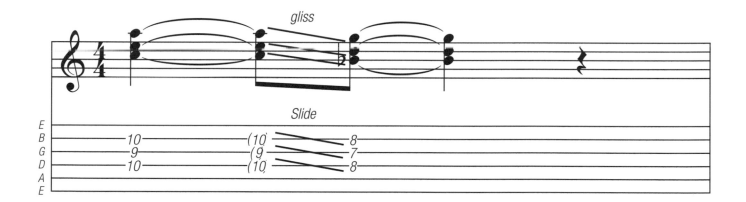

This kind of reasoning might not appear to be straight-out-of-the-textbook, good common sense, but the whole idea behind chord fragments is that they might not be complete chords. However, there is enough aural information there to suggest the chord voicing shown in context.

In this case, we've established that the key is C. It's quite likely that there's a bass player playing a root note and maybe even a pianist playing an outline of C7, too, and so you can be sure that this three-note chord fragment is enough to get the idea of C9 across nicely. Context again, you see.

Now let's look back at an old friend:

C minor pentatonic

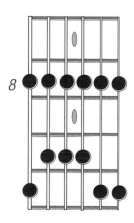

Its formula breaks down to this:

C min pentatonic = C E♭ F G B♭ C

          1 3 4 5 7 1

Neither a sixth nor a ninth in sight. So what happens if we now include these extra scale tones in our pentatonic model?

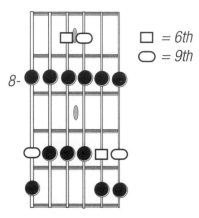

C minor pentatonic with added 6th and 9th

□ = 6th
○ = 9th

It's OK in that it works as a scale, but we're getting quite a long way from the original neatness and simplicity of the minor pentatonic in its original form. Plus, of course, I'm sure you're not looking forward to revising everything you've learned so far, adding these extra tones as you go.

I wouldn't do that to you, fear not. There's a much easier way to start integrating these new notes into the scale that requires virtually no further learning on your part at all...

The Major Pentatonic Scale

You might have heard of this particular scale, and if you have, you might have been wondering why I was keeping quiet about it until now! It's all to do with learning things in the correct sequence – and in accordance with our blues timeline – once again. It's vitally important to become acquainted with the basic minor pentatonic and to get the sound of that particular scale well and truly placed in your head before we challenge that knowledge with some more input, if you see what I mean.

Only after really understanding the minor scale from the point of view of shapes on the fretboard and sounds in the ear can you fully appreciate where these new notes fit in to the overall context of things.

So, without further ado, let's meet the new scale...

You'll no doubt be thinking that you've seen this particular critter somewhere before – and you'd be right. The wonderfully convenient thing about the major pentatonic scale is that it's exactly the same shape as the minor version, the only difference being that it begins on a different note. In other words, where C minor pentatonic begins here, at the eighth fret...

C minor

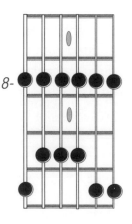

...C major pentatonic actually begins here:

C major

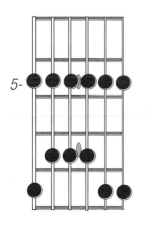

The only difference between the two is that the whole scale shape has slipped down the fretboard four inclusive frets.

What I want you to do now is to introduce this newcomer to your practice routine immediately by carrying out this simple exercise: every day, take any root note you choose at random and play the minor pentatonic from it, immediately followed by the major version from the same root note. Devise a way of making the choice completely random.

So, if the note you chose was A, here's how the exercise would run:

A minor pentatonic   *A major pentatonic*

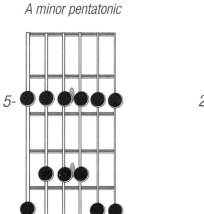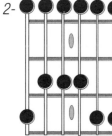

Alter the choice of root daily, but keep this exercise in your practice routine for a few weeks, as it's important, once again, for this information to be input to both the head and hands.

Here's a chart of all the major pentatonic scales, with the roots highlighted:

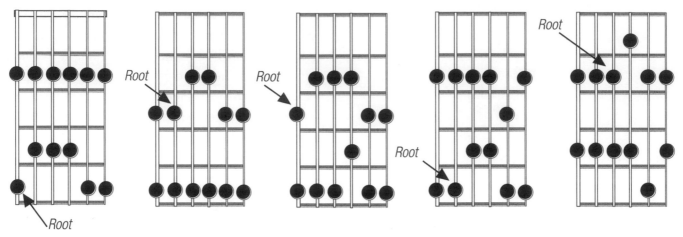

The five pentatonic major shapes showing the root positions

And naturally, this form of the pentatonic scale can be played in the 'horizontal' forms, too…

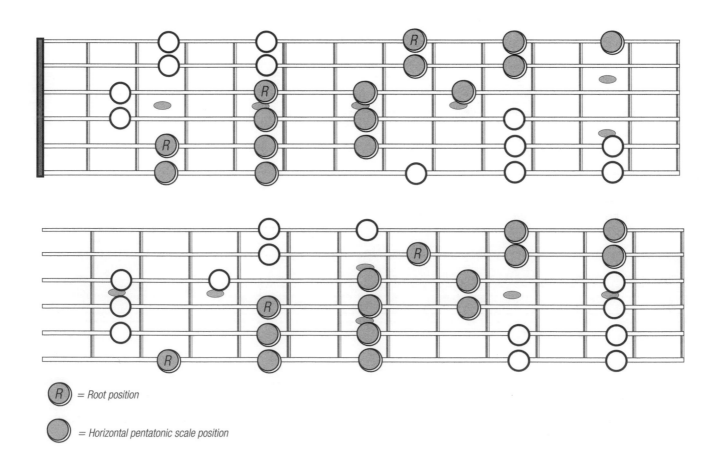

(R) = Root position

⬤ = Horizontal pentatonic scale position

It shouldn't take you too long to implant the new major scale into your practising; all the shapes are the same, as we've seen. It's really just a question of getting your ears attuned to the new sound with which they're being presented.

Once you're sure that everything is ticking along nicely and that you've reached a stage where you're confident with both forms of the scale and can find them in any key relatively easily, you'll be ready to move on – but not until then!

I used to test my students. I'd name a key and a version of the scale and watch what happened. For instance, I might nominate the following scale shape – in the key of D major – and watch them work out where this would be located.

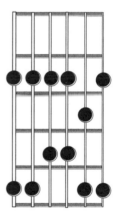

Most of them became accustomed to doing the mental arithmetic involved speedily, and I was sure that then we could start looking at some more practical applications of all the scale forms that we'd learned together.

So, submit yourself regularly to the same test – I won't be there to glare at you while you find the scale concerned, or to congratulate you when you find it instantly, but be fair with yourself all the same. When you can do the sum in your head quickly, feel free to continue with the next area of study. But please beware of the pitfalls I've already mentioned: those of impatience to rush ahead or frustration from working with the same materials over a long period of time. Rushing ahead won't get you any further along the line – remember, it can take years before you're fully comfortable with this kind of information, and so please don't ask the impossible of yourself. Patient,

persistent practice – the three Ps – is really the only way to make progress.

In fact, I used to write these words of wisdom on the board at every workshop I took: 'The answer's practice. Now, what's the question?'

It was uncanny how many times we'd find that the answer to any problem being discussed in class was, in fact, practice. I would be asked things like, 'How can I improve the co-ordination between my right and left hands?' and I'd ask if the student concerned had ever done any exercises that had been designed specifically to improve that particular area. The answer was no pretty much 100 per cent of the time, and so I'd show the class some simple exercises to improve their co-ordination and point out that, as usual, the answer was, indeed, practice!

Minor Blues

As we saw in the chapter on blues harmony, actual minor blues are comparatively rare and usually take on more of a rock feel and more straightforward song form – as in the case of the example I cited, Led Zeppelin's 'Since I've Been Loving You'.

Melodically speaking, here Jimmy Page was using a true minor scale for that famous intro; it's called the *natural minor*, or the *Aeolian mode*, if you prefer. (There are a couple of examples of this scale in different keys in the 'Scales Summary' section in the Appendix for your consideration.)

It's interesting to note that, while we can get away with using the blue third over what are effectively major chords, it doesn't work the other way around. The blue third actually sounds terrible over a minor chord and so, when dealing with songs of this nature, we have to suspend all our blues thinking temporarily, because an awful lot of our 'stock riffs' or 'phrasebook licks' won't work.

In order to handle a minor blues, you have to adopt a new discipline and avoid anything that clashes with minor harmony – like using the major pentatonic scale and the blue third. This is why it's a good idea to learn the Aeolian mode and use this as a sort of minor-blues resource. You can still play 'bluesy', and so nothing too dramatic has to change, you just need to avoid the mysterious third – another reason why I think minor blues tends to be more rock than blues. Take the blues third out of blues and what are you left with?

Like I say, minor blues are comparatively rare, but I've put an example backing track on the CD for you to experiment with, just in case you come across one on your musical travels...

Riff Blues

Remember when we were looking at blues harmony and I said that another form of accompaniment was available to guitarists in the Chicago and post-Chicago eras – ie, the *riff blues*?

Accompaniment riffs, or even blues that are based on a riff rather than a chord pattern, abound around this era. If you want a definition, I'd say that a riff accompaniment is what's happening on Cream's live version of Muddy Waters' 'Rollin' And Tumblin''. Listen to what Clapton's playing under Jack Bruce's wild harmonica and vocal lines.

The other type, where the riff figure actually forms the hard core of the accompaniment itself, is more like 'Killing Floor'. Compare the original to Led Zeppelin's version from *Led Zeppelin II* and you've got a potted history of how the development of guitar riffs were approximately linear to the development of more powerful amplification!

Riff accompaniment can be treated almost like chord arrangements, in a way. Instead of having dominant chords built on the I, IV and V of a key (in C, this would be the familiar C, F and G progression), the riff is based on the same roots. So you may start with a riff on C and, when the music would normally call for the chord to change to the F, the riff moves up accordingly. So you end up with a similar riff based on the three blues chord roots.

There are some examples of 'riff blues' on the accompanying CD. If the above thesis sounded a little complicated, check them out because I'm sure everything will become crystal clear at that point.

Oh, and there's one last point to observe where riffs are concerned: they are, of course, principally made up from pentatonic scales and chord tones, and so nothing dramatic changes from a technical point of view.

Using The Major And Minor Pentatonic Scales Combined

Right, let's see exactly what we've got when we fuse the two pentatonic scales together.

C minor pentatonic = C E♭ F G B♭ C
$$1 \quad 3 \quad 4 \, 5 \, 7 \quad 1$$

C major pentatonic = C D E G A C
$$1 \quad 2 \quad 3 \, 5 \, 6 \quad 1$$

Put them together:

Combination or maj + min = C D E♭/E F G A B♭ C
$$1 \quad 2 \quad 3 \quad 4 \, 5 \, 6 \, 7 \quad 1$$

Now this is interesting, because it means that we have created a sort of dominant-seventh scale, only with both types of third – and we've already agreed that the true 'blue' third is neither major nor minor, so that little anomaly is already taken care of.

C dominant-seventh scale = C D E F G A B♭ C
$$1 \, 2 \, 3 \, 4 \, 5 \, 6 \, 7 \quad 1$$

Combination or maj + min = C D E♭/E F G A B♭ C
$$1 \quad 2 \quad 3 \quad 4 \, 5 \, 6 \, 7 \quad 1$$

Very similar, aren't they? Neither of them contain the flat fifth, which is interesting, because we've already seen how important that particular note is to blues in general. If we do put it in, it confuses the exact nature of the scale's definition, because the 'blues fifth' is definitely a note that is totally independent of the natural fifth. This is unlike the 'blue third', which is nearly always midway between the major and minor, with few exceptions.

The two fifths, however, exist together.

Dom 7 scale with added flat 5 = C D E F G♭ G A B♭ C
$$1 \, 2 \, 3 \, 4 \, ♭5 \, 5 \, 6 \, 7 \quad 1$$

So this scale can't actually be called a 'dominant-seventh flat-five scale' from the point of view of strict textbook harmony, but it's about as close as you can get.

There are many ways of defining the blues scale, but in my experience there's always trouble when you start trying to apply pure, book-read harmony to blues. The point is, it was never meant to be pinned down and turned into an academic subject. As I said way back, the early blues guitarists didn't have a guitar in one hand and a music textbook in the other; there were no blueprints when the music first started; it evolved outside any plausible attempts to define it – at least from the point of view of Western harmony.

To this extent, calling it this or that is an argument not really worth having. I reckon that I could come up with at least three or maybe four different definitions of what the blues scale 'is', from the point of view of music science, but in the end, is it really worth it?

We end up by coming across more questions than it's worth answering, and so we might as well just get on with the job of playing the music and leave those of us who are perhaps more academically inclined to argue their socks off!

Enter The Mixolydian Mode

If we can agree that the scale I've outlined above will do as a perfectly passable collection of notes that will get you by with more modern blues, then I'll offer you another name to conjure with: the dominant-seventh scale is also known as the *Mixolydian mode*. You may have run across this term in other books on blues – you may have heard, for instance, that the Mixolydian is a good starting point for learning to play jazz. This is true, without doubt, but I would add that it's possibly the point at which blues stops and jazz carries on.

Modern blues players such as Robben Ford, who represent the 'jazz side of blues', go a lot further in their melodic explorations of the blues, and the Mixolydian offers a good basis from which to understand a little bit more about what's going on when they do. We won't concern ourselves with this just yet, however – our blues timeline hasn't quite stretched that far. I just thought it was worth introducing you to the Mixolydian and defining it for you, in case you'd come across it in the past and were wondering how it fits into the overall scheme of things in this particular book!

Using What We've Got

However we try to formalise the blues in terms of scale content or whatever, it's actually far easier to understand it if we use the minor pentatonic as a starting point, add to it the major pentatonic and get playing using this general pool of notes – at least until your ear has developed to the point where you can efficiently superimpose the two scales into a single position.

When we do this, all we end up with is the good old dominant/Mixolydian scale with a blue third and a flat fifth anyway – but if the sound of all these notes is inside your head, you're not going to worry about what scale, mode or whatever you're playing; you'll just be playing blues in the tradition of it being a folk music – just like the old days. It is, to my mind, a purer approach: the pentatonic scales are easier to handle, in general.

So let's take an everyday blues chord by chord and see what goes on melodically. First of all, let's start with a C7 chord:

$$C7 = C\ E\ G\ B\flat$$
$$1\ 3\ 5\ 7$$

And let's take a look at the two scales we can choose from in order to play a melody – or guitar solo, if you want – over the top of it.

C minor pentatonic = C E♭ F G B♭ C
1 3 4 5 7 1

C major pentatonic = C D E G A C
1 2 3 5 6 1

This brings us to an important point – I may even resort to using capitals for this, we'll have to wait and see…

A lot of people who are starting out, armed with the pentatonic scale and a blues backing track, believe that every note of the scale is equal and so they can practically randomise the scale over the chord and everything will sound OK. That's not so far from the truth, in fact, but I'll just tidy things up a bit and say that all the notes of the minor pentatonic scale will sound OK over the chord of C7 apart from the F – but certain notes will sound better than others.

Why should this be so? Well, if you think about it, if all you're doing over a chord is playing the notes that are contained in that chord, you can't make a mistake from the point of view of playing a wrong note, but the result is always going to be shapeless. A good melody needs direction and you can't get this from playing haphazardly; your solos need shape and we can learn all about this by acknowledging one simple fact: the notes of the pentatonic scale are not equal; there's a hierarchy!

Effective Soloing

The strongest note, in terms of a chord/melody relationship, is always going to be the root. In other words, the strongest note in our C7/C minor pentatonic relationship is going to be C. This represents 'home'. It's an incredibly stable-sounding note and, as such, is therefore a perfect foil for us to set up something that music depends upon, which is contrast. Light and shade, loud and soft, dissonant and consonant –

whatever you want to call it, music depends on this simple function in order to move along.

You can try a simple test: put on one of the backing tracks from the CD and go through it, playing only the root note of the chord in each bar. You should be able to recognise two things: it's as stable as a mountain, but it's as boring as hell at the same time! Try it with any other note from the chord and the effect is weakened; the result is not so strong. But it's still boring...

The reasoning here is that the root note is rock solid – it's the most appropriate note that you can play over any chord. It's boring because it's waiting to go somewhere else; melodically, you've got to leave 'home' and venture out amongst the other scale notes to move things along a little.

What's another good note to play alongside the root note? You could try another chord tone – and my suggestion is the third. There's nothing better (or more bluesy) than a blue third after a root.

So, over the C7 chord, try something like this:

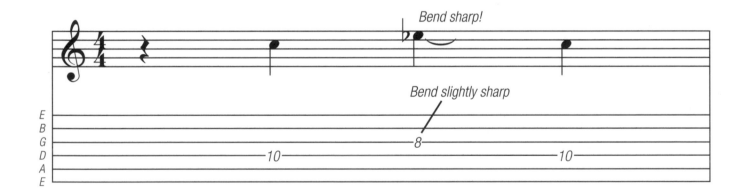

Sounds good, doesn't it? What's happening here is that you start off at 'home', move out in the open slightly and come straight back. It's almost like you're in a new neighbourhood and this is the first time you're leaving the house. You've really just stuck your head around the door and come straight back in – but musically speaking, you've been 'out'; you've made your first journey.

Now try the same experiment again, substituting any other two notes at random, and you'll find, once again, it doesn't sound as good. Certainly not as positive, in any case (I add this just in case you really

struck it lucky and played something that sounded fantastic by accident!).

Referring back to the root in the way that we did the first time around sounds like a positive statement – something of musical value – and this is because we have begun to observe the basic laws of melody. We're anchoring the melody to something strong – the root note, in this case – and the effect is quite dramatic.

Naturally, when the chord changes, 'home' changes. And, once again, the root note of the new chord provides us with the focal point for any melodic exploring that we want to do.

Staying in C, the second chord would be an F7, so with this chord you could play something like this:

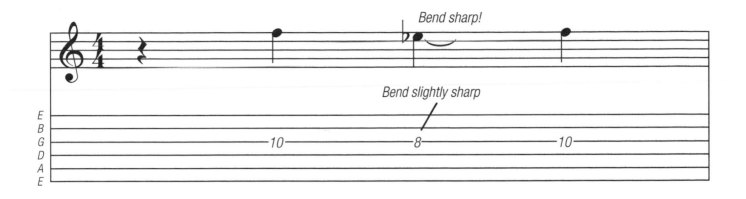

Once again, all that's happening is a peek around the door, musically speaking, but as a phrase it works and has all the strength and character of the C7 version.

There's a track on the CD that just changes between C7 and F7 for you to practise this particular exercise (and, naturally, for your own melodic exploratory experiments), so spend a little time with it.

To recap, you'll be playing this:

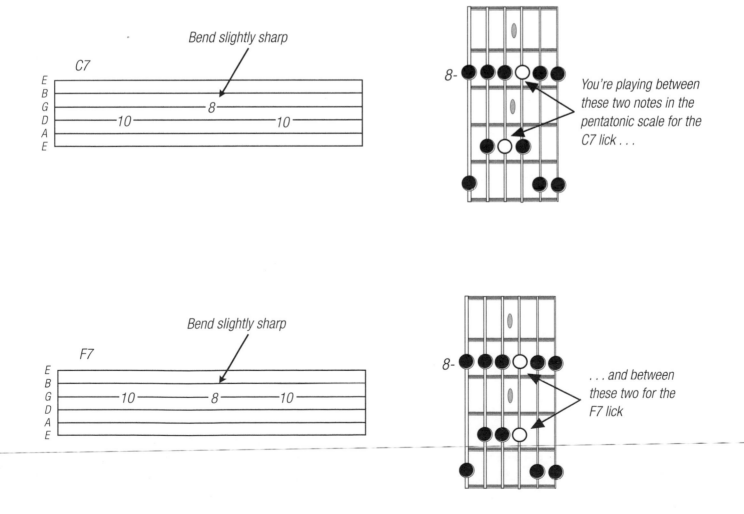

Next up in a C blues is G7 – and the system stays in place exactly as before. If you play something like this...

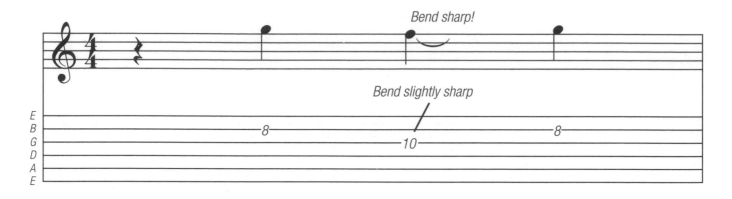

...you can't go wrong.

Notice, incidentally, that we're not doing exactly the same thing each time, from a musical point of view. All that's really happening in these initial forays into blues melody is that we're playing root notes and their immediate neighbours – really sticking close to home in familiar territory each time. If we wanted to, we could play a similar phrase each time; in other words, you'd be playing root and blue third each time, giving everything a nice uniformity. Let's look at what happens here:

$$C7 \text{ chord} = C - E\flat$$
$$F7 \text{ chord} = F - A\flat$$
$$G7 \text{ chord} = G - B\flat$$

Spot the odd man out? The $A\flat$ doesn't belong to the minor pentatonic, and yet the phrase works in the context of the chord. Curiouser and curiouser. But we don't really have to look too far for the answer. In each case, we're talking about the root and blue third, and we've already determined that a blue third is slightly sharper in pitch than can be notated in our system of writing music. The blue third lies between two neighbouring tones.

So, if we write out what's happening again, making all the right allowances, let's see if it changes anything:

$$C7 \text{ chord} = C - E\flat/E$$
$$F7 \text{ chord} = F - A\flat/A$$
$$G7 \text{ chord} = G - B\flat/B$$

This makes everything agree because, whereas $A\flat$ might not be in either the major or minor pentatonic scales we're currently dealing with, the note A most definitely is, and so we're actually on far more solid ground than might at first have been apparent.

That's why this phrase doesn't sound as bad as it could in other music situations where playing a note not in the scale is a risky enterprise, especially in your Freshman year! (You could be accused of being a jazz musician, for instance...or worse.)

Now, you'll probably agree that, if all our soloing ideas were as organised as the two ideas we've looked at so far – and you must agree that, while they weren't exactly amazingly interesting, they nevertheless worked better than the 'shouting and pointing' approach I spoke about earlier – we'd be off on the right foot. And, of course, this is exactly the state of affairs we want to bring about.

Ear Training

Most of what happens from here on in is down to introducing the ear to the concept of note hierarchy and 'safe houses', 'focal points' and the concept of 'home'. Your fingers already know their way around the terrain of the fretboard, but now you need your ear to guide you through.

This was a thing that happened naturally back in the days when music was handed down purely by ear. The fact was that students of the blues in the early days became naturally very good at playing by ear, because they had no choice. So their musical ears developed as a natural part of their learning to play – something that doesn't happen today.

Now, it's quite possible to pick up the music or tab to a piece of music and polish it to a shine without understanding any of it from a musical point of view. And, what's more, the ear never really has to become involved: learning music has become a purely visual thing – read it and play, paint by numbers. But there really is no substitute for training your ears, musically speaking. They are the best friends you've got on the bandstand. Remember this: a £7,000 guitar won't help a pair of 50p ears!

A great many of the problems that students bring to me in lessons or workshops can be put down to poor ear training. A good set of ears will help you out in any number of areas, especially the following:

- phrasing
- note selection
- tone
- playing with emotion
- improvisation

And more besides. How many times have you heard a guitar teacher say that part of your practising ought to include listening, not just whiling away your time playing scales and exercises, but inputting music to the brain? Remember, all the information we've looked at so far is no good to you if it isn't in both your hands and your head.

I listen to music all the time. If I have to learn anything, whether it's a specific tune or just a style of playing, I'll listen to the same thing day after day. In the past I've even gone to the lengths of recording several tracks I'm trying to learn and taking them with me on my daily commute into the office. (This was obviously when I worked in an office. These days I just turn left when I come out of the bedroom and I'm there!)

During an interview with a blues musician once, I asked what sort of advice he'd pass on to people who were learning to play the blues today. His answer was immediate: 'You've got to listen to the music you love. Sing it in your head if you can't actually play it, but keep listening to it, because one day it's going to start playing back through you.'

I've never forgotten that – and what's more, I've proved it to myself on a number of occasions when I've played something that I don't ever remember actually learning; it's just filtered its way through somehow from head to hands.

Becoming A Better Musician

Where do we start? Realistically, all we've got to do is follow through with what we've been looking at so far, but be knowledgeable of the fact that this particular section of our training concerns the ears and not just the hands.

Returning to our C blues idea, you've been practising playing the little root-related phrases over the changes on the CD (I hope). Now we're ready to take things a stage further, but a few words of explanation may be necessary first.

After the root note of a chord, the other strong points are its chord tones. After all, these are the notes which fit over the chord better than any other – right? So we can't exactly go wrong; it's just that the result may not be too inspired. Let's look at the chords in a C blues and their respective chord tones:

$$C7 = C \; E \; G \; B\flat$$
$$F7 = F \; A \; C \; E\flat$$
$$G7 = G \; B \; D \; F$$

All of these chords can be played using a single arpeggio shape.

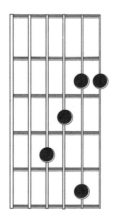

Play it at the eighth fret for the C7, the 13th fret for the F7 and the third (or 15th) for the G7. This particular arpeggio involves playing the root, third, fifth, seventh and root again in that order, a method that helps the ears appreciate things a little better.

If you play along with the C blues backing track on the CD, you should be playing something like this:

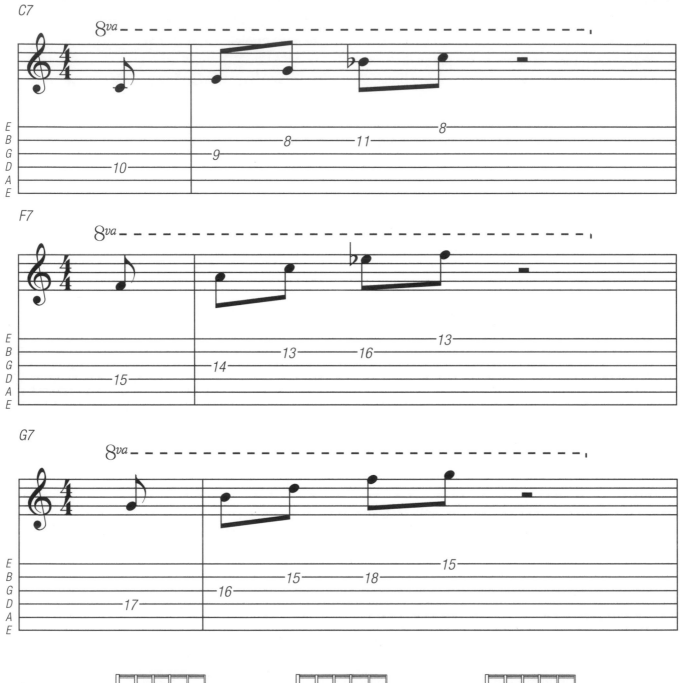

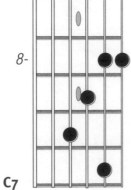

C7

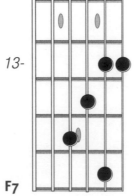

F7

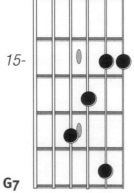

G7

You should notice two things immediately: everything sounds 'right' and in its proper place, musically speaking, but it doesn't sound like a solo as such, more of a rhythm part – and of course it does. You're only repeating the harmony in the form of single notes, in any case, and so it's bound to sound like an extension of the rhythm part, rather than an exciting, original solo. That comes later; for now we've got to let the ears know exactly where all the safe spots are before we can let them loose in the neighbourhood.

This particular exercise insists that you change position between chords in order to keep the dominant arpeggio exactly the same shape. In practice, of course, this isn't desirable or practical (although, as a pure exercise, it's not a bad one for keeping you in trim), and in the end you'll be playing far more economically as things sort themselves out over time.

If you like, you could play the same exercise using these shapes:

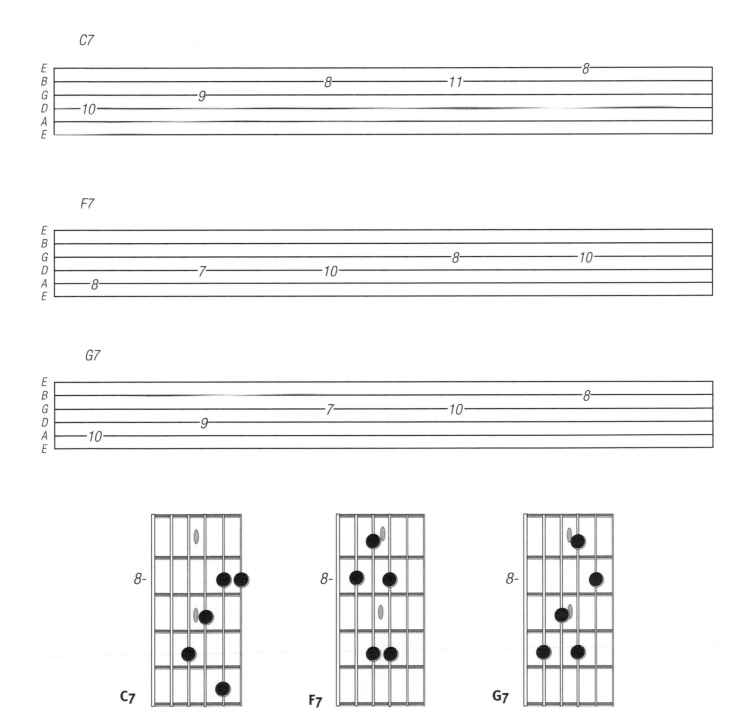

You'll lose a certain amount of uniformity, but at least it gets things concentrated in a smaller area and imitates more accurately the sort of space you'll be working in later on.

One interesting thing to think about while we're here is the question of playing 'the perfect solo' over any given piece. I've had this particular discussion with many students and musicians in my time and we've agreed that there is a tendency to forget one vital thing: a song's melody was its original and best solo! In other words, nothing fits any given chord arrangement – blues or anything else – quite like its original melody. Another fail-safe method for soloing, therefore, would be to learn to play the melody and, if all else fails, stick really close to it while you're playing your solo. The audience won't think you're cutting corners; they'll probably think you're just being a bit of a smartass!

Next Steps

I'd recommend that you keep the arpeggio exercise we've just looked at in your practice routine for a few months just to make sure that the information is being well and truly embedded in your ear. You don't need to spend hours on it; just once a day will keep everything oiled nicely.

This type of exercise has a very gradual effect, but after doing it for a while, you might find that you can 'hear' things on records a little more clearly. By this,

I mean that you might be able to begin to pick the odd thing up here and there from other guitarists' playing. (I'm going to tell you how to study other players' licks and styles later on, incidentally.) This is all well and good and demonstrates to you that your ear is doing well.

The next step is to start experimenting with the minor and major scales we've been looking at. In order to make things simple, I'd suggest that you actually limit yourself initially in terms of the notes and scales you experiment with, as this will help to develop your phrasing.

For example, I used to get my students to perform what I call the 'three-note guitar solo', which means that you pick three notes from one of the scales – usually these...

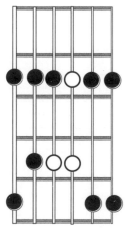

...and make a solo up from phrases drawn from these three notes exclusively. You could use something like this:

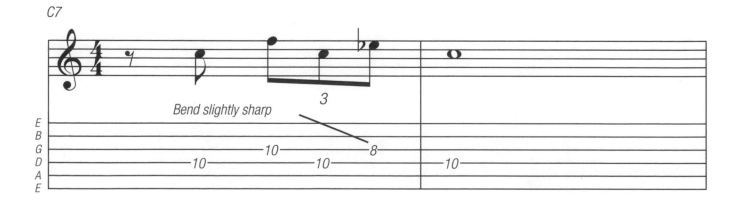

Or this:

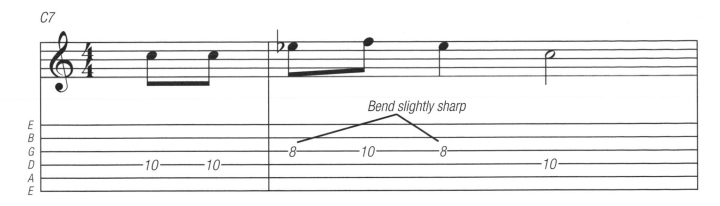

In effect, anything that sounds good will do nicely. What we're doing here is taking away one of the more bewildering aspects of playing a solo: that of having a whole fretboard of notes to choose from and not really knowing where to start. By deliberately cutting out this part of the process, you get a chance to take a good listen to what you're playing in a limited field.

> 'Albert King was my other hero. I did "Cross-Cut Saw" on my album. I really tried to capture his tone. It seemed like he had one lick and he turned it around sideways, upside-down, and played all these variations on it. But it was all the same lick!' *Leslie West*

Every time you find a phrase that works, write it down. Keep a book with loads of tabbed-out ideas in it and review them all occasionally. This way, you'll start building up your own 'phrase book'.

Again, it makes a great deal of sense if you think of music as being similar to learning a language. After learning some essential vocabulary, we begin speaking short phrases long before there's any sense of overall understanding or fluency.

Remember, first things first. You won't be able to take long improvised solos in the early years of playing because you need the kind of fluency that comes only with time and practice. In much the same way, you wouldn't expect to be able to hold a conversation in a foreign language if you were still very much at the 'phrase book' stage.

Working From Tabbed Solos

Ideally, when you reach the stage of full-blown experimentation with the scales over backing tracks, you should try your hand at some new material every time you practise.

We're lucky (in a way) that virtually everything of any significance ever played on the guitar can be found in a transcribed form somewhere. There are literally hundreds of books available which claim to be note-for-note versions of albums. There are also magazines that regularly transcribe blues solos and, if you can't find what you're looking for in a shop, you can bet that it exists in some form or other on the Internet!

So there really isn't any excuse for not inputting some new material into your practice routine at very regular intervals.

Incidentally, I said above that we're only lucky that all this material exists 'in a way'. I must temper this statement by adding that I think that transcribed solos have actively prevented a lot of guitar students from developing their ears. Studying tabbed solos is perfectly fine as long as it's put into the context of an overall practice plan which includes some form of ear training.

Trying to learn music solely from numbers is missing the point. Without your ear directing you, your playing isn't going to pick up on the emotional side of music at all, in much the same way that painting by numbers isn't a good way to go about studying art.

So please make sure that this area of your study is backed up by some ear training – and we're going to look at one sure-fire way in a moment or two. First, let's go cherry picking...

Cherry Picking

I've seen many students get completely lost with transcribed solos: they run out of enthusiasm because it seems to be taking too long, or they can't get past the awkward bit in the middle, and so on. So I developed this idea that I call *cherry picking*, which means that you don't have to learn the whole piece – and you certainly don't have to spend weeks trying to perfect something that is still technically too hard for you at this stage in your development.

It's a good idea to get the chord arrangement under your fingers – that sort of thing ought not to be beyond you, as long as you've spent your time in the trenches, learning your chords and attaining a certain level of athleticism on the guitar neck.

In general, it's very good to attempt material that you find slightly tricky at the outset – but this has to be balanced with common sense. Don't try things that are still technically too far in the distance for you; this will lead to frustration and you'll probably end up giving up. The smart way is to lead yourself forward in measured steps and give yourself achievable goals.

Cherry picking basically means that you go through a transcribed piece and pick out the phrases, licks and riffs from a solo or rhythm part that appeal to you, then isolate them from the piece and study them.

It's even a good idea to copy out some of them into the book you're keeping for your own discoveries. Run through all of them every so often and tick off the ones that you've perfected.

Cherry picking means that you can cover quite a lot of ground reasonably quickly. What's more, by taking phrases from many different players and reassembling them in your own playing, this means that you're beginning to build a style for yourself. A player's style is usually a result of all his influences coming together, being allowed to simmer gently for a while in the practice room and then served up anew in a different context.

'I always had a very eclectic musical palette. Everything from mainstream radio – y'know, Stax and Motown – to Skip James. And for me, it was natural that it reflected itself in my performing. But the trick was getting it to the point where it wasn't just playing musical ping-pong; it was something more cohesive.' *Eric Bibb*

Learning Licks From Records

Another great source of material is sitting there waiting for you in your record collection. Presumably, such a collection comprises music from artists who inspire you, and so the easiest way of saving yourself the trouble of hunting down transcriptions would be to dig the good stuff out for yourself.

Of course, this sounds like a huge task to undertake – I've met people who are completely floored by the transcriber's art – and yet it's one that's not too hard to master to a useable degree, and it's a fantastic facility to have on board.

Years ago, back in the early blues era, songs and guitar styles were worked out by ear, as nothing was written down. It meant that a musician had to develop an aural facility early on in order to get themselves some sort of repertoire. As we've seen, this current generation has tabbed solos to lean on, and this has perhaps had the effect of tempting many students away from developing their ear to the extent that it can indeed become their best musical friend. (I know I keep repeating this, but it is something I feel really strongly about, so please humour me!)

'I had nobody to tune my guitar and I couldn't watch the television to see what the guy was doing. I had to try to figure out what he was doing!' *Buddy Guy*

Both blues legend Buddy Guy and jazz-guitar great Tal Farlow told me the same story: they would learn licks from listening to the radio. When they heard something they wanted to 'steal' from a recording, they would pick up their guitars and try to play it straight back. After years of hit and miss, they both managed to develop this facility to quite a high degree, meaning that their ear training was complete – and at the equivalent of black-belt level. But one pass was all the time they got to get the lick from the radio. Otherwise, they'd have to wait and hope that the DJ would play the record another day. It must have been like ear training under fire, but look at what it gave them in return.

Of course, I understand that it's not easy to make the leap from avid listener to active transcriber, but these days there are some helpful little doodads on the market to lend a hand while you develop your chops in this area.

You may have heard of phrase trainers already. These are gizmos that you can buy, plug a CD player into and record around 20 seconds of any one particular track and slow it down. Now, here's the clever bit, because, thanks to digital technology, you can now slow things right down practically to stop if needs be and keep the recording to pitch. This means that you can slow down a riff or lick and listen to it played back to you note for note, as slow as you like, but at the right pitch.

When these things came onto the market, they revolutionised certain sectors of the transcribing field. At last you could be pretty sure that everything you wrote down was 100 per cent accurate.

There are a few of these pocket wonders on the market at varying prices, but, owing to recent developments in computer software, it's now possible to download programs that will do exactly the same thing – even in real time, if so desired. The best I've found – and one I use myself – is called Transcribe! and is available from www.seventhstring.demon.co.uk. You can download a free 30-day evaluation copy from this site for either PC (boo!) or Macintosh (hoorah!) computers, and it's simple and intuitive to use. Simply convert a CD track to an MP3 file, launch it into Transcribe! and you're off. The program even gives you best-guess scenarios at chords, and so it really is a transcriber's dream, especially if your ear still has a way to go before it can pick things up at full speed.

I really would advise everyone to have a go with something like this. If you don't get on with it, at least you'll be doing your ear some good while you're playing with it. And if you do pick it up, there won't be a lick, solo or riff on record that you can't hoover up and recycle in your own playing.

'I've tried to come up with some guitar playing which is as devoid of cliché as it can possibly be. I'm really not interested in getting on stage and playing Albert King licks.' *Walter Trout*

Review

So the plan is as follows:

* Familiarity with minor and major pentatonic scales all over the fretboard, in both 'horizontal' and 'vertical' positions;
* Graduated work with backing tracks;
* Study from transcribed solos;
* Cherry picking
* Learning to take things from recordings via hardware or software.

If the above steps are followed, everything should develop nicely with your playing and you should find your facility as a blues guitarists growing noticeably.

Where Jazz Meets Blues

'I don't believe in playing things the way they have already been done, especially when they have already been done well! If you don't put your own thing on it, you're rehashing somebody else's style, and that's pointless.' *Robben Ford*

Where to next? I suppose that our timeline has now reached the point at which blues and jazz again meet, at around the late '60s and early '70s, and decide to pair off. The result was termed *fusion*, and from a blues standpoint, the music took another change in direction.

At workshops, I often hear names like Robben Ford, Larry Carlton, Lee Ritenour and so on coming up when we talk about players who have taken blues beyond its basic pentatonic capabilities. Of course, blues is nothing new to jazz players – they've been playing their own interpretation of blues for years. It's just that it carries with it a far richer tonal and harmonic vocabulary.

You remember when we found the sixth and ninth both cropping up in the blues, and so we integrated them into the blues scale? Well, we have to do a similar task here in order to cover the musical expertise of the players I named above and others like them.

It's a thing that lies well beyond the focus of this book – it really is better to come to the blues with a jazz perspective rather than the other way around, and so that's possibly another book I'll have to write someday! But I will take a couple of paragraphs to outline what happens when these two musics join hands.

Let's just remind ourselves about the particular scale tones we've already agreed upon for use in blues:

$$C \quad D \quad E\flat/E \quad F \quad G\flat/G \quad A \quad B\flat \quad C$$
$$1 \quad 2 \quad \text{blue3} \quad 4 \quad \flat5/5 \quad 6 \quad 7 \quad 1$$

As I said earlier, this is a contentious point and various academics are bound to challenge me to a duel at sunrise over it, but I'm satisfied that this is the basic, fully functioning blues scale – in essence, at least.

Now let's look at what tones are available to us from the chromatic scale:

$$C \quad C\sharp/D\flat \quad D \quad D\sharp/E\flat \quad E \quad F \quad F\sharp/G\flat \quad G \quad G\sharp/A\flat \quad A \quad A\sharp/B\flat \quad B \quad C$$
$$1 \quad 2 \quad 3 \quad 4 \quad 5 \quad 6 \quad 7 \quad 8 \quad 9 \quad 10 \quad 11 \quad 12 \quad 1$$

Jazz is a very chromatic music and makes full use of the chromatic scale via passing tones and what's generally referred to as *extended harmony* (see Chapter 4, 'Blues Harmony'). In other words, a jazz player will embellish the basic I–IV–V format of the blues to include extended dominant chords that make use of the flat and sharp ninths and the sharp and flat fifths, too. We know that any chord tones used in the harmony tend to end up being used in the melody, too, so it's no surprise that jazz players will use this enhanced vocabulary in their solos as well.

If you're prepared to make the journey towards understanding all the ramifications of the blues in jazz, then, as I've said, it's best to approach it via the study of jazz, rather than blues. You'll hear players talk about whole-tone/half-tone scales, the 'altered dominant' scale and many more besides. Personally, I think there is an easier way to look at things, if all we want is a taste of what's happening. Take the ordinary pentatonic scale...

$$C \quad E\flat \quad F \quad G \quad B\flat \quad C$$
$$1 \quad \flat3 \quad 4 \quad 5 \quad 7 \quad 1$$

...and move it one fret to the right:

$$C\sharp \quad E \quad F\sharp \quad G\sharp \quad B \quad C\sharp$$
$$\flat9 \quad 3 \quad \sharp4 \quad \sharp5 \quad \natural7 \quad \flat9$$

You've instantly got a scale that includes some pretty shady characters – melodically speaking – all of which wouldn't be out of place in the playing of some of the jazz-based bluesers.

The trick with jazz is to resolve a line correctly – once again, landing on a root or chord tone will do nicely – but what you do from your point of departure to when you arrive back 'home' can be as chromatically enhanced as you like. Musicians refer to this as *outside playing*, which doesn't mean that they've been sent out to the garden shed to practise, but playing outside the scale.

I'm not going to pretend that the strategy I've outlined above is anything like a method for playing jazz blues, but it might serve to show you the very basic idea behind it. As a friend of mine once remarked, jazz is all the wrong notes in all the right places!

Conclusion

As far as our blues timeline is concerned, we've moved from the somewhat humble beginnings of the stark minor-pentatonic scale, in the days before the riff or guitar solo, right up to a 'jazz' point of view of the blues. In doing so, we've added tones, expanded our ideas on the fretboard and discovered how to input new data at a constant rate.

The rest is down to more study, taking an individual player's style and looking at it in extreme close-up, seeing what's there and extracting what we think is useful to you. On this score, there are any number of videos and DVDs available which offer serious insight into artists' playing styles and techniques.

Now that we've got DVD technology with us, more concert footage is available in this medium, which offers zoom, slow-motion and freeze-frame facilities. Any information you can lay your hands on that will help you understand more about the music – or the techniques behind the music – will help to embellish your own knowledge and increase your potential as a musician.

6 BLUES TECHNIQUE

'Know the song first, the words and what it means to you, and then the guitar will come in behind it. I don't think that the guitar is more important than the song. So, if you can accompany the song and enhance the words, then that's the best technique.' *John Hammond*

There's absolutely no doubt in my mind that a poor sound on the guitar is a result of poor technique and, thereby, a large part of the answer to our 'What's the problem?' question.

It's not necessarily the student's fault – we live in a time when a lot of people choose to learn in isolation, sometimes purely from tab, and they don't set out to practise pure technique in its proper context. It comes down to the old story of not really knowing how to practise – or even what to practise – to enable the technical side of your guitar playing to come up to scratch.

The thing is that you should practise techniques like string bending and so on with as much enthusiasm and within the same time scale that you'd allow for practising an actual piece, song or solo. Good technique doesn't come overnight; it develops slowly and, if it's not properly addressed, it won't have a chance to develop at all.

There are two main reasons why technique remains elusive to guitar students: one is that technical exercises are boring, no matter how much good they are destined to do to your playing, and the other is that it's difficult to know exactly what to practise anyway.

Surely just playing helps your technique to develop? Well, no, it doesn't. Poor technique will remain poor until it's corrected somehow. For example, if your string-bending technique is generally inaccurate, in that you either underbend or over bend – in either case, the result is something woefully out of tune and bad-sounding – no amount of playing is going to help correct it. And yet some simple exercises within an effective practice routine will put things right in a fairly short period of time.

To put it another way, practising technique helps your playing in a very general sense, whereas practising single pieces or songs are very specific – and if your technique isn't up to scratch, everything will continue to sound bad.

Here's The Deal

When I was teaching one-on-one, I used to make a bargain with my pupils: I used to tell them that we had an hour together and, out of that hour, the first ten minutes of the lesson were mine, during which time we'd do some technical exercises, play some scales and generally make sure that their technical engine was ticking over nicely. The rest of the lesson was theirs and we could do anything they wanted. If they wanted me to show them a song or write out a solo, that's what we did.

To my mind, this took care of two essential elements: one was monitoring their technical development on the instrument, the other was nurturing their musical style. In other words, I'd act as their coach and encourage their general musicality to grow and help them to avoid some of the blind alleys that are rife in music.

I want to strike a similar bargain with you: I'm going to set out a few exercises that will aid you in acquiring some key areas of technique. The good news is that you haven't got to spend hours doing them over and over; all I'm asking for are the first couple of minutes of your daily practice routine, nothing more. This should guarantee that the exercises never become boring, but they will help you slowly and surely over a period of time. First of all, we'll look at a vital area that covers just about everything we're going to look at...

How To Practise

This tends to be an area that is never seriously looked at during the long slog of learning the guitar. The majority of pupils I've taught have had very bad practice habits which have resulted in a sort of learning 'black hole' – they put an awful lot into it but never get anything back!

Space And Time

First of all, I encourage everyone to take a really good look at the environment in which they're intending to practise. To get the most out of it, you need to create a space that is conducive to learning. The corner of a bustling living room in which a lot of other people are involved in doing their own things – watching TV, doing the ironing or whatever – is practically useless. You really need peace and quiet and, preferably, solitude.

I realise that this ideal is difficult to achieve, given the geography of the modern living space, but if you can't find a quiet space, it must be possible to find a quiet time at some point during the day, when everyone else is off somewhere doing their own thing. Just half an hour's practice in a suitable environment will pay dividends that just cannot be achieved by practising all the right stuff in the wrong places.

Posture

It's a sad fact that a lot of guitarists end up with poor posture, owing to bad habits in the practice room. A great number of players seem to suffer back problems and a lot more make the whole job of learning that much more difficult for themselves by sitting in the wrong position.

If you don't get fundamental things like posture right in the early days, you'll end up with limitations built in to your playing style. As a fairly mild example, a couple of well-known players say that they can't play barre chords. They're not telling us this just to cheer us up a bit by exposing an Achilles heel in their otherwise sublime technique, either; it's something

that perhaps hasn't held them back, but it obviously worries them in some small way, otherwise why mention it? But I guarantee that, if you take a look at their posture, you'll find out why barre chords remain out of the question. It's usually down to wearing the guitar impossibly low on a strap, meaning that the conventional barre technique of placing the index finger across all six strings would be an impossible task for the left-hand wrist to perform (try it, by all means – but please don't hurt yourself!).

They get around the problem by using their left thumb over the top of the neck to block the strings and achieve a similar effect to that of the ordinary barre. Once again, if you experiment by holding your guitar neck low enough for your left arm to remain practically straight, you'll see that the thumb is in a far better position to perform barring duties than the index finger ever could be. It works, but it doesn't make this deviation from the norm something that might work for you, so please don't copy what is essentially poor technique; if you start off down the right road, where this kind of thing is concerned, you stand a far better chance of achieving your playing goals. Develop some bad habits later on, by all means, but for now, let's take the well-trodden path!

So what is the correct posture? For a start, I'd warn you against one of the common problems I see with students, which is actually having two postures: one for practising and the other for playing. I can always tell if I'm looking at a player who has spent most of his playing life sitting down (ie practising), because he looks awkward standing up with his guitar on a strap.

I used to get students coming up to me saying, 'I can play it sitting down, but I tried playing it in rehearsal last week and I couldn't play it at all!' This is all to do with incorrect posture in the practice room and can be eradicated by acknowledging a simple rule from day one: practise in the same position in which you're intending to play.

Try this simple experiment: adopt a comfortable position with your guitar sitting down – in much the same position as that you would adopt when you practise. Play something you know well and then put a guitar strap on your instrument and play it again standing up. If everything falls to pieces the second time around, you'll need to make a simple adjustment to how you're sitting.

But first, repeat the process, and this time take a look at the different positions the two playing postures bring about. The chances are that your left hand was lower or higher when you were sitting down, for a start. Well, that's two different positions that you've got to learn to play in, making the job twice as hard. It's a little like learning the piano standing up and then someone suggesting that you sit on a bar stool to play.

You'd be surprised at how picky classical players can be about playing position. Pianists fastidiously alter the heights of their stools before performances in order to ensure that everything is as familiar as possible for them. In other words, they try to reproduce in performance the conditions under which they learned to play and perfected the piece in the first place. Trying to play in any other position is making the whole process unnecessarily hard.

Classical guitarists, too, insist on chairs of a certain heights and types in order to bring about the same set of circumstances. Some even go to the extreme of taking a chair on the road with them. They're not being finicky; they're just making it easy on themselves.

It's a very good tip to adjust your guitar strap so that the guitar falls naturally into the same position when you're either sitting or standing – and to wear it for both practice and playing.

Don't Waste Time

Most of the pupils I've taught have admitted to me that their practice time tends to be undisciplined and fairly directionless. When I suggest that the norm is that they sit down, play everything they know and then put the guitar down again, I usually get the feeling that I've hit the nail squarely on the head!

But of course, unless you are regularly exposed to material you can't play, where's the challenge that will help propel you forward? It's only by pushing the boundaries of your technique and musicality that you can ever hope to move further on.

So the keyword here is *organisation*. Try to organise your practice time so that you are dealing with specifics. An ideal practice routine might be split into three areas:

- Warm-ups and technical exercises
- Learning some new material
- Playing through your repertoire

Taking these sections one at a time, let's start with the warm-up section. This kind of thing is essential – no one can expect to start playing at their best from cold. Even the top professionals warm up before a performance, just like an athlete before a race will do some stretching exercises to make himself ready.

I suggest that a few minutes of scales and various fretboard exercises – preferably accompanied by a metronome – should form the basis of these precious first few minutes of your schedule. You'll certainly be better prepared for section 2, that's for sure...

By 'new material', I mean anything that is new to you. It might be that you're in a band and you need to learn some new songs, or merely that you want to work through a transcribed solo. It can cover a whole range of things.

Even if there is no imperative for you to learn a specific piece or solo, try putting something unfamiliar in front of you and working through it. Play the chords, or look at the riff or a couple of key licks from a solo. It's only by placing yourself in unfamiliar territory on a regular basis that you pick up some of the essential instincts you'll need as a player and performer. One of the most important of these is, of course, that being confronted with new material won't freak you out!

Put it this way: if you're used to looking through songbooks and playing the chord arrangements virtually from sight, you're going to find playing in a band or at jam sessions far easier to cope with. New material or the unfamiliar in general isn't going to give you the same problems as it would if you weren't used to looking at this kind of thing in the practice room.

The third section can also carry a fairly broad brief. By 'playing through your repertoire', I mean having some fun: put on a backing track and play along or polish up something that was previously in section 2. Anything that involves 'playing' as opposed to the slow slog of 'learning' will fit nicely into this particular slot.

Of course, all of the above are mere suggestions. Everyone brings their own agendas to learning the guitar, and you might have some specific needs outside the ones I've outlined above. But the message is always the same: these days, time is often limited, as far as things like guitar practice is concerned, and so don't waste it. Make a plan and stick to it!

Be Regular

Another thing that is a very good idea but is, in practice, quite hard to bring about is the idea of practising at the same time every day. It's the same sort of advice they give people who are training – athletes and so on: it's far easier to make practice into a habit if it becomes part of a repetitive daily routine.

This also has another valuable built-in feature in that you actually start feeling guilty if you miss a practice session – which, when you think about it, is going to help you in the end, however annoying it might be at the time!

Pure Technique

When we talk about technique in isolation, we're not talking about what notes you're playing; we're really considering how those notes are played. It would be wrong to consider technique as being something cold and clinical; the idea of the super-fast picker standing on stage reeling off endless, unspirited, emotion-free solos is a particularly tired cliché.

Music isn't some sort of track event – competence in any art form can't be measured using a stopwatch. If that was the case, there'd be classrooms full of English Literature students trying to work out how fast Shakespeare could write – in other words, seriously missing the point!

I look at technique from the point of view that it is seriously beneficial to a player's overall style: it should help him or her play the music they want to play. Brought down to basics, technique should help you to get the notes out.

A parallel here would be that good typing technique doesn't make you a better writer, but it makes the job of writing that much easier.

It's commonly thought that blues isn't a very technical music, mainly because of its supposedly humble beginnings. Surely the originators of the blues weren't great technicians? Well, once again, I'd direct you towards the historical blues collections available on CD. You'd be surprised at just how many of the early blues guitarists actually had quite polished technique (particularly the rag players from the '20s and '30s).

So, exactly what needs to be done in the practice room in order to address the question of technique? For a start, we'll take the two hands separately, starting with the left hand.

'It's down to the touch and sensitivity of the player, and the phrasing and the space that you leave. It's all those things.' *Gary Moore*

Left-Hand Techniques

One of the main advantages we guitarists have over pianists (for example) is that we have much more of a chance to 'form' the notes we play. There's something in the fact that we never really lose touch with the string – certainly with the left hand, in any case – that allows us more breadth of expressiveness.

Certainly, this is one of the key elements that gives a player an individual style – give two guitarists the exact same instrument, through the same amplifier, and you'll end up with two completely different sounds. It's a bit like handing a pencil around a room filled with 20 or so people and getting them to write out the same phrase; the content would be the same in each case, but the handwriting would differ enormously. And that's what we're really working on here – we want to initiate the process whereby you can develop your own musical 'handwriting'.

Vibrato

Vibrato is one of the most important techniques to develop for a guitarist – and it's the one that takes the longest to perfect.

After all the hundreds of seminars I've done, poor vibrato technique remains the chief suspect if someone tells me that he's not happy with his 'sound'. It's nothing to do with instruments or amplifiers, types of string, pick-ups or whatever; it usually begins with what's going on under the individual's fingertips.

If anyone seriously suspects their gear of letting them down in any respect, I always get them to try this simple test: unplug the guitar and listen to what you're playing at a pure acoustic level. If everything sounds right there, then look for problems further down the line (pick-ups, amplifier and so on). I must admit, it's usually the case that we stop at this primary stage and agree that the acoustic sound isn't too hot in the first place.

There's a nice story that I heard about this belief that it's the guitar/pick-ups/amplifier that gives you a good sound. The great guitarist Chet Atkins had just given a show somewhere in the US and a fan had come backstage to talk to the man. He looked at Chet's guitar, sitting on a stand in the dressing room and said, 'That guitar sure has a great sound!' to which Chet replied, 'Doesn't sound so great now, though, does it?'

I've told that story at workshops before to really ram home the idea that good technique equals good sound and that there isn't a make or model of guitar or amplifier that can turn a poor sound into gold, and yet I still get students coming up to me saying, 'Your guitar sounds really nice. What pick-ups are you using?'

One particular time I took the cheapest guitar I could find along to a workshop and played it through a really cheap amp – but I still wonder whether the point ever really got across. So, one last time before we look at vibrato in detail...

Good technique = good sound

Basically, there are two types of vibrato available to guitarists: there's the subtle classical guitar style and the more 'bluesy' style. The difference begins with exactly how we move our fingers on the string.

Classical vibrato involves moving the fingertip along the string, like this:

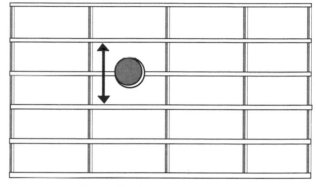

Classical vibrato

This results in putting just enough movement into the string to give the sound a slight contour. If you liken vibrato to 'sound modelling', then I suppose classical vibrato is just enough to smoothe out a few of the rough edges and nothing more. In fact, it can almost sound like tremolo (which is technically a variation in volume; the term *tremolo arm* is completely wrong) if it's done a certain way.

Blues vibrato, on the other hand, is different in that it involves a side-to-side movement with the string:

Blues vibrato

The difference between the two in terms of sound is almost immediately apparent, and both are useful as 'sound modelling' tools, so let's look at them both in even closer detail.

Classical Vibrato

In order to perfect the classical version, begin working on it very slowly and practise only this technique and nothing else.

For this part of your practice routine, focus exclusively on producing a smooth, even and sweet sound from the instrument. I would also counsel you to practise this acoustically, either on an acoustic guitar or an unplugged electric. This way you can be sure that the sound you're making is the direct result of flesh on metal and wood and not anything else further down the line.

Pick a spot on the guitar neck around the seventh fret and put your index finger down on the string – here, for instance:

then your top E to see this contrast in action) and position on the neck, so getting it to sound right in one place isn't by any means doing the whole job. Experiment with the other fingers on your left hand, too; ideally it should be possible for you to add vibrato to any note played by any finger – but take measured steps and be prepared to spend time at each stage.

You needn't devote too much time to practising vibrato; just a couple of minutes at the beginning of your practice routine should do nicely. Just remember to practise vibrato and nothing else for the time allotted.

Blues Vibrato

The method for practising blues or 'side-to-side' vibrato follows almost exactly the same rules. Start in the same place...

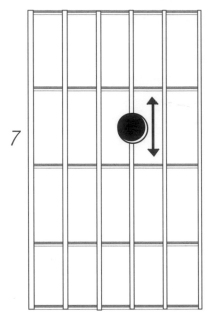

Pluck the note, move your fingertip very slowly from left to right and, above all, listen to what happens. You should hear something like the slow vibrato example on the CD. Use this as your target sound and don't move any further forward until you have a workable foundation sound to begin with.

A lot of the movement necessary actually comes from the wrist, not the fingertip – and definitely not the elbow, as I've seen in some extreme cases! You're not shaking the whole arm overmuch, either; try rocking the wrist to move the fingertip.

Next, pick some different locations on the neck and repeat the exercise. The amount of movement you add to the string varies depending on where you are on the neck – for example, the strings feel stiffer and more resistant down near the nut, and so you have to adjust your technique accordingly.

This is another thing that I don't think a lot of guitar students recognise: there isn't just one vibrato technique that you can apply liberally all over the neck; it actually changes very slightly depending on thickness of string (try adding vibrato to your bass E string and

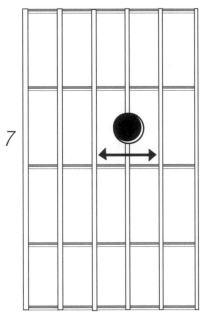

...and very slowly move the string from side to side. The wrist comes into play here, too; I've likened the movement to turning a door knob before now. The wrist rotates slightly – more so here than for the classical type of vibrato.

Once again, listen to the CD for a target sound and have patience. Good vibrato chops don't happen overnight; it can take years for a player to achieve a good vibrato technique. But one thing is for certain: you'll never achieve a good sound unless you focus on it exclusively for short, regular periods.

Once you're satisfied that your slow blues vibrato is sounding good, move on to the next stage outlined above: change location, string and finger and repeat the exercise until you have smooth, even vibrato. Keep it slow – discipline yourself severely here. It's very tempting to rush ahead and speed things up prematurely, but it won't do you any good. We're aiming to build solid foundations, and rushing the job could have disastrous effects on your sound.

Only when both your classical and blues vibrato techniques start sounding good at a slow pace should you even consider speeding either of them up – and, when the time comes to do so, take it a few degrees at a time. Don't go from a standing start to full speed ahead in one leap, or you'll potentially be damaging all the work you've done so far.

Move forward slowly and set yourself reasonable, reachable objectives. By this, I mean that saying things like 'I'll perfect my vibrato by next Tuesday' is right out. It's going to take a lot of time, but if you address the situation each and every time you sit down to practise, you'll see results.

There are some examples of medium-paced vibrato on the accompanying CD, and these should become your new targets after the initial spadework has been done. There's nothing to adjust from a technical point of view – it really is the same movement with the fingertip speeded up in both cases.

When speeded up, your new watchword will be *control*. Don't stiffen up: everything you do on the guitar should be with the arms, wrists and hands as relaxed as possible. Tension anywhere here will slow you down and could possibly lead to strain injuries, so remember to keep things as relaxed as possible at all times. Short-term improvements in your playing are not worth longer-term injuries.

As long as each stage is taken slowly and you remember to focus on nothing but your vibrato technique for a few minutes each time you sit down

to practise, there should be nothing preventing you from achieving full-speed vibrato in the long term. One last thing, though: don't try to add vibrato to a bend before you're ready!

String Bending

This is another technique that causes a lot of people to have nightmares in the early stages of their development. It's another area which can affect the sound of your playing enormously – an out-of-tune bend is pretty excruciating to listen to in anyone's book – and yet, if things are taken slowly from the word *go*, there's no reason why this should ever develop into a weak area in your playing.

If you think about it, string bending is just another way of moving from one pitch to another on the fretboard. It's thought that the whole technique was born because early blues players were trying to recreate the sound of the voice, which was their first point of reference for blues melody.

This is one of the reasons why pianists have such a comparatively hard time when playing blues: they can't *gliss* (that's musicspeak for slide) between notes – and they certainly can't bend them! – so a great deal of this original nuance in blues melody is unfortunately lost.

We guitarists, on the other hand, have the means to bend notes pretty much whenever we like, which is probably one reason why the guitar remains the dominant blues instrument (unlike jazz, where guitarists are relegated to third place behind pianists and sax players).

The first steps in efficient, tuneful string bending rely on one very important factor: knowing your target. It's all very well applying the mechanics of string bending to a note that you choose, but, in every case, knowing when to stop bending is a key factor. Therefore, you can go about pulling your bending technique into line by using the tried and tested means of focusing on bending for a few minutes each day and taking your time.

Let's start with naming the parameters. We need both start and end points for our bend. For the example over the page, we'll take fret 7, string 3 as our starting point.

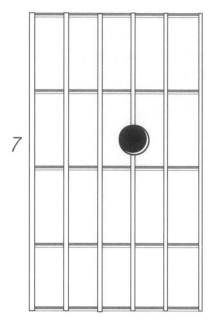

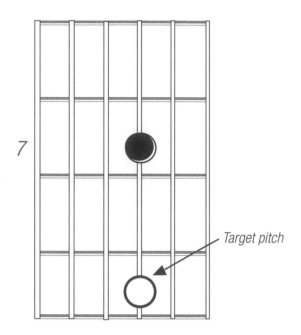

Target pitch

This is going to be a bend from the note D to the note E on the G string. That's a two-fret/full-tone bend, as shown in the diagram on the right. Take care to get the bent note in tune:

The next step is to sound both notes (the D, followed by the E) and then – and *only* then – place the third finger of the left hand on the D, laying the rest of the fingers behind it to support the bend, like this:

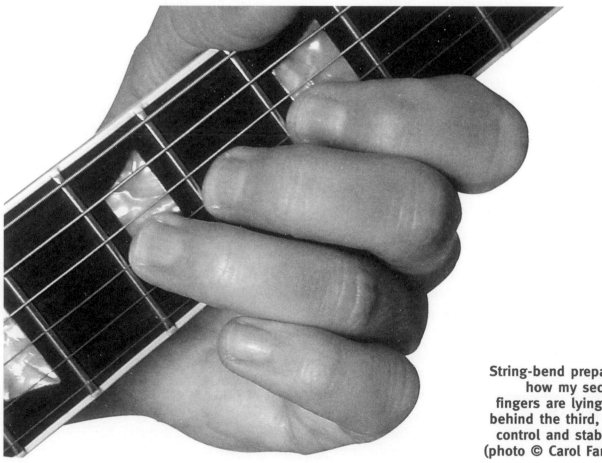

String-bend preparation. Notice how my second and third fingers are lying on the string behind the third, ready to help control and stabilise the bend (photo © Carol Farnworth 2003)

Now, push the string over towards the bass strings – *slowly* – until your ear tells you that you've reached your destination pitch. You should end up with something that looks like this:

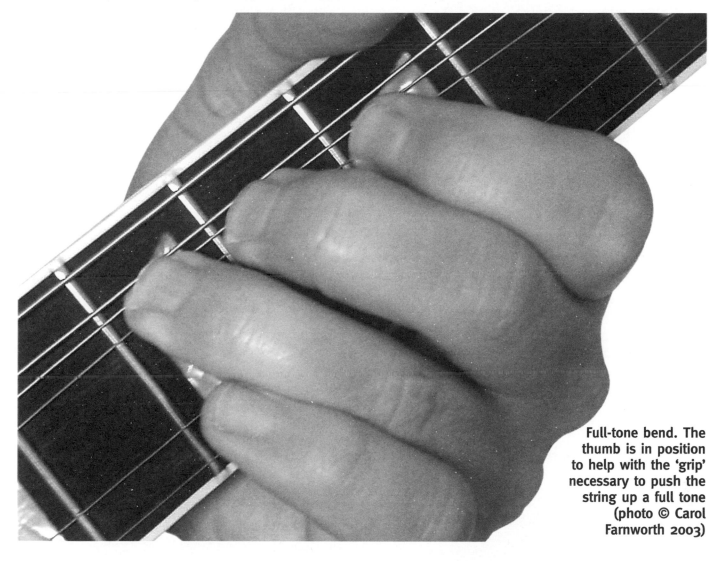

Full-tone bend. The thumb is in position to help with the 'grip' necessary to push the string up a full tone (photo © Carol Farnworth 2003)

Now, this is enough to be going on with to begin with; repeat this exercise for a minute or so every time you practise and don't take it any further until you can hit your target note square in the middle every time.

The next step is very similar to what we did when we were looking at vibrato – try the exact same exercise at different points on the guitar fretboard because, just like vibrato, bending feels considerably different depending on where you are on the guitar's fretboard. Bending the second fret on the G string (ie the note A) up a tone to B – which is a similar distance to what we were doing in step 1 – feels very different because the string is more difficult to move down at this end of the neck.

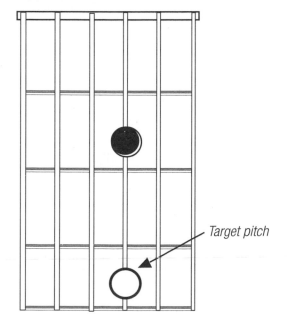

Target pitch

Try the same trick up an octave, between the 14th and 16th frets, and not only does the string feel a lot looser, you don't have to push quite so far.

So, as with vibrato, you can't get by with perfecting your bending technique at one place on the fretboard and hope that you will be able to apply the same set of rules universally. Criteria such as string size and fret location all have an influence over what the bend will feel like under the fingers, and so you've got to move this little exercise around for it to have the full effect.

Once you're good at hitting the target at several points on the fretboard, you can try the exercise again using your first finger. The idea is to start exactly as before: place your first finger on the third string, seventh fret (top diagram) and give yourself an aural idea of your destination fret (bottom diagram).

All you then need to do is push. The first thing you'll notice is that it feels a lot more difficult to push the string with the first finger than it did when you were trying the same thing with the third finger.

Think about it: you haven't got the same amount of push with your third finger, owing to the physics of your left hand. It's a different type of movement, too: whereas before you were using the first and second fingers to help the third finger push, this time the first finger is out there on its own. You can't call on the wrist for too much help, either; the first finger has to pull, as shown in the photo opposite.

Initial reaction from students I've taught over the years when trying first-finger bends has usually been 'Ouch!'. Yes, it does hurt a bit to begin with – especially if you're still relatively new to the guitar and your left-hand fingertips haven't hardened up yet. However, stick with it, because it gets easier as you go on.

Next, follow the same path with the first finger as you did with third-finger bends: more of the same at different locations all over the neck until you can just about hit your target note every time.

People ask me if they should be able to bend with all their fingers, and I'm afraid the answer is yes – even the little one! But it's definitely the first and third fingers that come in for most of the bending work, and so it's here that we spend most time locked in the woodshed.

The next step is to try to bend other intervals – to give yourself different target notes, in other words. You could try any semitone/one-fret bend like this:

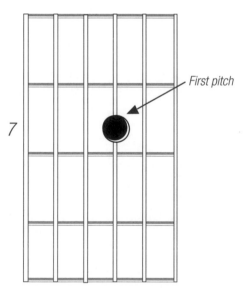

First pitch

7

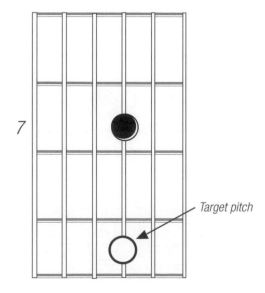

7

Target pitch

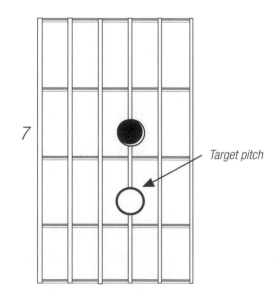

7

Target pitch

First-finger bend. Let's not beat around the bush: this actually hurts the first few times you try it – but art is pain, after all... (photo © Carol Farnworth 2003)

Or even a minor-third/three-fret bend like this:

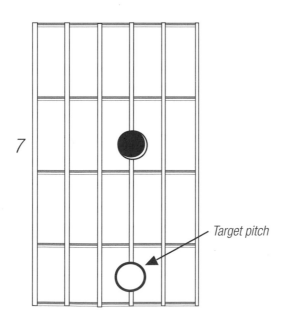

Target pitch

Whatever you try, the rules are the same: practise bending in isolation, focusing on it exclusively. Identify your start and target points to give your ear all the

information it needs to send the correct commands down to the fingers – and take things slowly.

If you follow this plan to the letter, I can practically guarantee you success with your string bending, which will do an awful lot for your overall competency as a blues guitarist.

Reverse And 'Silent' Bends

I want to throw in just another word or two about the idea of 'pitch targeting' as far as string bending is concerned. Obviously, I can't over-stress the importance of the ear in almost every aspect of your playing – it is, after all, the musician's most vital tool – but there's a type of bending that calls for the ear to take a step back and literally let your sense of touch take over.

You may have heard of a *reverse bend* or a *silent bend* somewhere – possibly it's been an instruction during a tabbed solo or something. Naturally, there's no such thing as bending a string down in pitch – unless you do it with a trem bar, of course. That's not quite what 'reverse' means in this context; it means that occasionally a note needs to be bent before it's played (there's an example on the CD if you're not sure what I mean).

In order to carry out this little manoeuvre, you must bend the string silently first, and the resulting effect is that of a bend in reverse – hence the terminology used to describe it.

You don't need me to tell you that your string bending has got to be very accurate if you're going to be able to pull this off – but you won't be able to rely on your ears; this is where your experience has got to take over and guide you through.

Try this little experiment: bend your B string up a full tone/two frets from the fifth fret. Your target note here will be the pitch at the seventh fret. In effect, you will be bending from the note E to F♯:

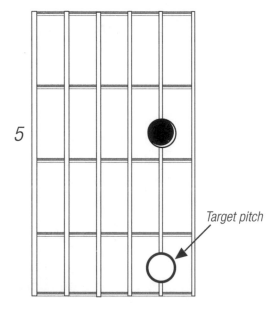

Target pitch

Now go up an octave to the 17th fret and try to bend up a tone to the F♯ once again. You're still bending between E and F♯, it's just we've gone up an octave in pitch and moved the exercise up the neck by 12 frets. You should be able to notice immediately that you don't have to bend quite as far here and that you're meeting less resistance from the string, and so it feels easier.

Now, imagine you have to do exactly the same thing again, but this time effecting a silent bend. In order to judge that you've reached the correct target pitch to begin with, you're relying on how the string feels under the fingertip – and this is different between the two locations.

Try a few more bends – still in octaves at this stage – on the other strings and you'll see that it's different for just about every string/location on the fretboard, and so you might begin to see how important it is to have done your homework correctly with the bends you can actually hear before starting to do any conjuring tricks!

In other words, a reverse or silent bend is a technique you can really only hope to master fully when your overall string-bending technique is fully up to scratch.

Bending With Vibrato

Surprisingly, this is actually more difficult than it seems. It would be tempting to think that all that's involved would be the simple task of putting two previously learned techniques together in a sort of sandwich – a simple fusion or superimposition. But you'd be wrong.

This is another key area of frustration for guitar students – the two things might work independently of each other, but the minute that you attempt to combine them, it sounds like a tricycle race in a room full of cats...

The trick here is down to the old adage 'slowly but surely' – and, of course, following our general plan of isolating the technique and practising it for a couple of minutes every day.

As before, we'll start with the familiar bend on the third string, seventh fret, bend up a tone to the E at the ninth fret and then try to add some movement to the string in order to bring about a nice, even vibrato. Seeing as this is the first bend you tried when we were looking at bending in general, this feat should not only be familiar to you, it should be 100 per cent on target!

Once you've reached the correct target pitch, relax the bend slightly before returning it the previous 'full-bend' position.

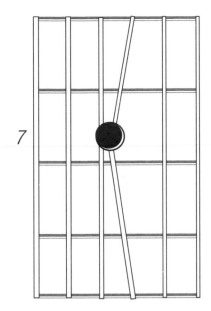

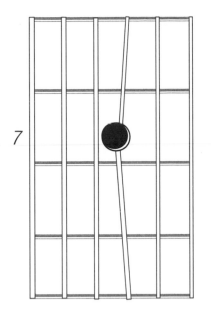

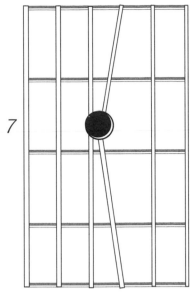

1: Bend the string to your target pitch   *2: Relax the string slightly*   *3: Return to your target pitch*

Listen to the slowed-down bend/vibrato combination on the CD for reference. Start slowly so that you're really sure of the mechanics of the technique before you start to bring it up to speed.

Gradually speed up over a period of time – if both techniques have been properly addressed previously, the act of putting them together should be something of a balancing act; you'll just need to sit there and make a few minor adjustments, but the correct sound will be in there somewhere.

Then, once everything is working – and don't rush things, as this could take a few weeks before it starts to sound right – move the technique over the fretboard as before to make yourself aware of how you have to adapt to different string thicknesses, degrees of bend, string resistances and so on.

Multiple-String Bends

Occasionally, you'll find it fun to bend more than one string at a time – although to begin with you might be wondering exactly how this might be possible. Needless to say, it's not a thing that you ought even to consider attempting until your bending skills are at a fairly advanced stage.

Multiple-string bends usually involve only two strings and are confined to points in the blues or pentatonic scales where two notes lie parallel to one another, like this:

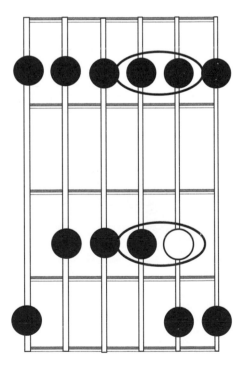

'Double stop' bends sound good where scale tones lie on parallel strings

Once again, it's down to either the first or third left-hand fingers to bear the brunt of multiple-string-bending duties. It's a case of grabbing both strings together, either with finger 1 as a kind of part barre...

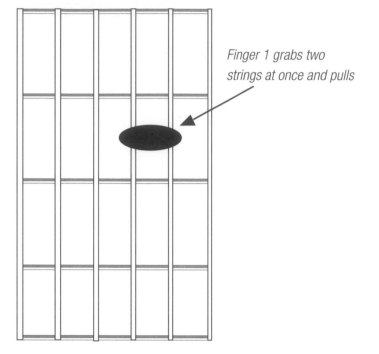

*Finger 1 grabs two
strings at once and pulls*

...or using fingers 3 and 4, like this:

**Multiple-string bend. Fingers 3 and 4
synchronise together to push the
strings up in a semi-harmonious way
(photo © Carol Farnworth 2003)**

To make a good sound with a multiple bend, you have to be aware of a couple of things, one being that strings don't tend to bend together in perfect tune. You're far more likely to get in the ball park than get things spot on target, in other words. But this needn't necessarily sound bad, as I've demonstrated on the CD.

My advice here is the same as always: don't attempt anything unless it's been well and truly experimented with in the practice room first. Take it slowly, pay it

your undivided attention at least once a day and don't expect immediate results. Soon, though, you'll be doing train whistles and everything.

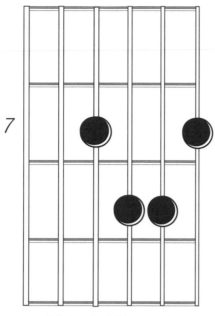

A 'train whistle' bend starts with a ♯♭ shape…

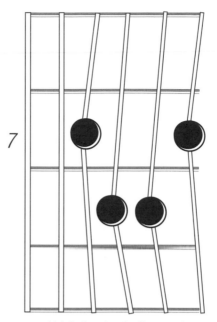

…which is then 'pushed' up on the fretboard to achieve the desired effect

Back in the pioneering days of blues, harp players (that's bluesspeak for 'mouth-organ players', incidentally) used to have to perfect a good imitation of a train whistle before anyone took them seriously. Guitarists could get in on the act, owing to the fact we can bend notes, too. So, practise the above example and all aboard!

Hammers And Pulls

The techniques which have been known for years as *hammer-ons* and *pull-offs* really come under one banner, known as *slurring*, from a technical point of view. Both can help your phrasing and generally give your playing a more rounded edge.

As we saw in the previous chapter, 'Blues Melody', solos are made up from scales – and I think we're agreed now that a player's touch and feel have an awful lot of influence on his resulting sound. Hammers and pulls are no exception, and both are fully representative of the 'less is more' principle.

You've probably spent hours working on your picking in the practice room, and hopefully you're beginning to achieve good co-ordination and a high

level of accuracy. But both of these techniques actually ask you to back off with the pick and let the strength and agility of the left-hand fingers take a bit more of the strain.

Let's think about it: when you pluck a note, you're hitting the string with a bit of hard plastic, and so every note has a 'peak' at the beginning, dynamically speaking. In fact, if you looked at a picked note from the point of view of a pure waveform on one of those clever machines they have in science labs, you'd end up with something that looks like this:

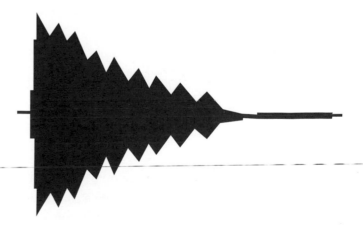

And, equally obviously, if every note in a phrase had the same sort of attack to it, you'd end up with a whole mountain range of peaks and troughs – agreed?

The result, in terms of sound, could end up sounding like you were running your thumbnail along the teeth of a comb – a sort of *rat-tat-tat-tat-tat*. Dynamically speaking, this isn't particularly attractive to listen to, and so we tend to try to smoothe things out a little by slurring some of the notes into each other, which leaves us with an audibly more satisfactory 'mountain range'.

Hammering On

Hammering may sound a little violent, but this is one of those techniques that is in use all of the time and so it's an important one to master. Once again, it becomes even easier still if you isolate it and spend some time focusing on it during your practice time.

Hammering effectively gives you multiple notes from a single pick stroke. Let's call on our test area once again and give it a shot. Place the first finger on the seventh fret, third string, and pluck the note. Immediately afterwards, swing your third finger onto the fretboard at the ninth fret:

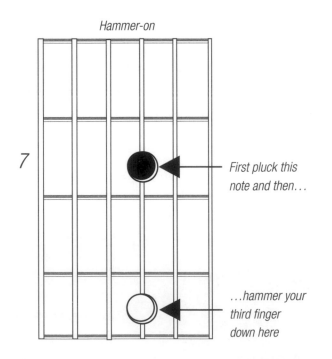

Hammer-on

First pluck this note and then…

…hammer your third finger down here

What should happen is that you should have heard two notes of similar volume coming from a single pick stroke. If not, some minor adjustments will have to be

made in terms of weight and force of the 'hammering' third finger. Keep trying until you hear two smooth notes from the single pick stroke. (There's an example on the CD for reference if you're not quite sure what things should sound like.)

After you're sure that things are proceeding according to plan, try the same technique all over the fretboard. It won't differ quite as much as bending did as you move across strings and to different fret locations, but it's good to be sure.

Finally, when you're really sure that you've earned your black belt in hammering technique, try giving multiple hammers a go, whereby finger 1 frets the note and fingers 2 and 3 – or even 3 and 4 – do the hammering so that you end up with three or four notes from a single pick stroke. This will take some working on to perfect.

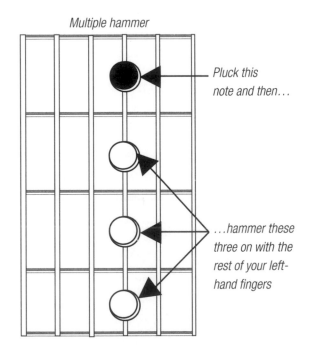

Multiple hammer

Pluck this note and then…

…hammer these three on with the rest of your left-hand fingers

As with all of these exercises, take this one all over the fretboard, getting used to the different sounds at different locations on the fretboard as well as the slightly different techniques required actually to produce them.

The Advanced Hammering class entails being able to hammer on to an unplucked string and produce a clean note, like so:

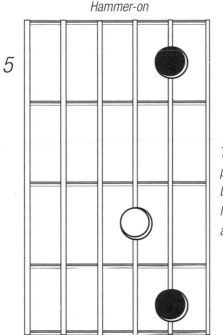

Hammer-on

5

The black notes are played with the pick, but the white note is hammered on 'cold' and unpicked

Pull-Offs

A pull-off is the exact opposite of a hammer-on. This time, you pick a note and pull off to a pitch below. Let's start at the usual place: put your third finger on the ninth fret on the G string with your first finger behind it at the seventh. It's important that the first finger is already in position and making good contact with the string and fretboard before anything else happens, because this is the note that will sound second in sequence.

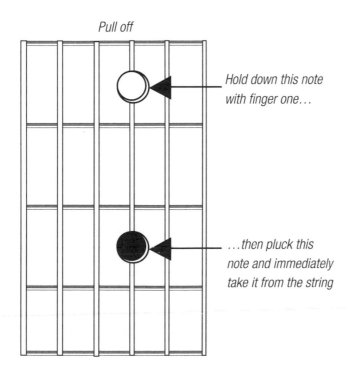

Pull off

Hold down this note with finger one…

…then pluck this note and immediately take it from the string

Next, pluck the note under your third finger and lift it off the string immediately. What you should hear is, once again, two notes of approximately the same volume from a single pick stroke. What might have happened, however, is a complete damp squib, inasmuch as the second note that you've pulled off to is of a much lower volume, or even hardly there at all. In this case, you might find that you have to pull the third finger off slightly sideways, so that the fleshy tip of the finger moves across the string, almost as if it was plucking the note itself.

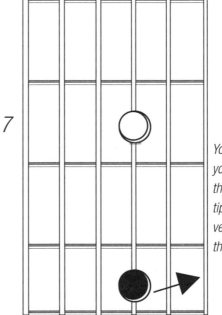

7

You may find that you need to catch the string with the tip of your finger very slightly to help the string sound

It's all down to experimentation in the practice chamber, exactly as before. You might have to play with different levels of pressure as you drag the third finger off – but remember, you don't want to do this with so much force that you end up with another 'plucked' note. That would spoil the effect and we'd be right back with the original spiky mountain-range effect.

Leading on from basic pull off technique, we follow the exact same path as before: try pulling off at different points on the fretboard, using different strings, etc, until you feel confident enough to try the 'multiple' pull-off, where you can get up to four notes from a single pick stroke.

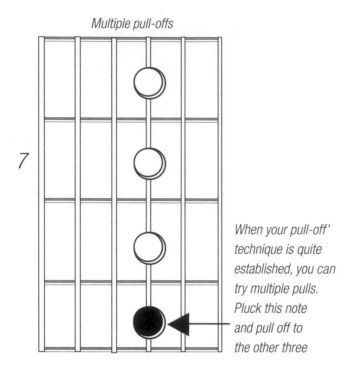

Multiple pull-offs

When your pull-off' technique is quite established, you can try multiple pulls. Pluck this note and pull off to the other three

When both techniques – hammering and pulling – are well up to strength and feel completely natural to you, try playing a few of the scale shapes you'll find in Chapter 5, 'Blues Melody', and see how economic you can be with your pick-to-note ratio!

Combining Hammer And Pull Techniques

If we combine the two techniques of hammering and pulling, we end up with something known in music as a *trill*. In order to do this, begin by playing a hammer, follow it with a pull, but then immediately hammer-on once again and repeat this for as long as your hand can stand it. This is a technique used a lot by players, such as Jimi Hendrix and Jimmy Page. It's at the edge of accepted 'blues' technique, but it's included in a lot of contemporary blues.

In a combination hammer and pull only the first note is plucked!

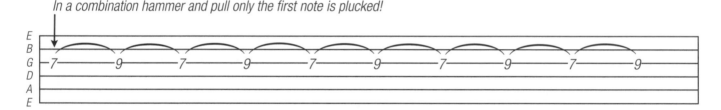

Sliding

In effect, this is a technique for slurring two notes together, but instead of hammering or pulling, you slide the note along the fretboard after plucking it.

Take notes D and E at the seventh and ninth frets on the G string, place your first finger on the seventh fret, pluck it and slide to the ninth fret, like this:

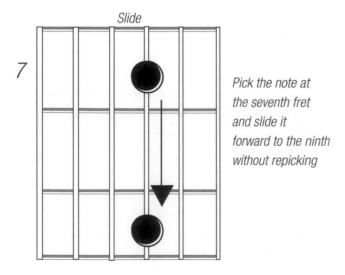

Slide

Pick the note at the seventh fret and slide it forward to the ninth without repicking

I've given you an aural clue on the CD so that you can check yourself against it. Experiment with it in both directions, sliding up and down. After you're really confident (and I usually find that students need their brakes looking at when they first try this technique – they either don't slide far enough and stop short or go way too far and overshoot), try increasing the distance along the string you're sliding.

The full use of this technique can be seen primarily in position changing. You'll see from Chapter 5 that there are five positions for all the scales we use on the fretboard.

One way of playing scales is to work across the fretboard, from one side to the other. But what happens if you want to move along the fretboard, rather than across it? This is where sliding is put to full use – not all the time, obviously, but it's one of the principal ways of relocating yourself on the fretboard. There are some great riffs and licks to be heard that include slides, too.

Finger Rolls

This might sound like some kind of macabre form of buffet, but in fact it's a very economic way of using the left-hand fingers, particularly the third...

You'll have noticed that many scales feature notes that lie at the same fret on parallel strings. This is particularly true of the pentatonic scales, which are pretty much the mainstay of playing blues.

You might want to try fingering two notes like these by using different fingers (as shown in the diagram opposite), or even by using the third finger in both locations. If a melody line, solo or riff calls for a quick or repetitive interchange between the notes, however, a *finger roll* makes a good alternative. This is a technique where the third finger plays both notes, by rolling the finger over from one location – almost like placing a part barre – to fret the other as well.

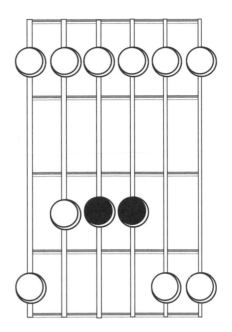

This technique calls for a certain amount of flexibility in the fingertip, so it takes time to develop.

Finger rolling. The top of my third finger has 'collapsed' to cover both third and fourth strings – a very useful technique if you're playing a rapid lick between parallel positions (photo © Carol Farnworth 2003)

Where finger rolls really come into play are on licks like this one, where the third finger would be otherwise much too busy swapping strings for there to be any sense of fluency maintained.

The only way that you'll ever be able to execute a good finger roll is – guess what? – by isolating the technique and just practising passages like the one shown above until the clockwork is sufficiently well oiled to produce results.

Do bear in mind what I said about flexibility, though: if you can't do it at the first attempt, don't think that it will never happen, because it will, once the fingertip has achieved the correct level of movement.

As I said, the third finger is possibly the most handy for this particular technique, but the first finger does its fair share of finger rolls, too. This tends to be easier, because the first finger is probably used to the idea of barring and so doesn't have the problem of adapting itself.

Once practised, this is a splendid technique for organising runs and smoothing off some rough edges in your soloing.

Left-Hand Muting

We're going to be looking more seriously at string muting in a few paragraphs, when we look at right-hand technique, but I thought it was worth stopping to consider how the left hand can be employed here, too.

Basically, some sort of muting is vital on the guitar practically all of the time. It's the only way that you can have any kind of control over the duration of independent notes and chords, especially in rhythm parts.

The left hand is called upon to act as 'string damper' every so often – when the right hand is too busy playing a complex picking or strumming pattern, for instance.

There are two main ways in which the left hand can be called upon here: one is merely to lift the fingers from the fretboard just enough to damp the strings

and create a sort of musical 'thud' rather than a note or chord; the other is literally a case of using whichever finger falls free to deaden the strings at will.

It may sound a haphazard process, but I'll go into more detail when we discuss right-hand damping a little later on.

Tools Of The Trade: Plectrums

Before we start looking at right-hand technique, a word or two about plectrums and string gauges...

Over the years I have noticed at a lot of seminars that I have given that people turn up with totally unsuitable picks. As you probably know, picks are measured in terms of their thicknesses in millimetres. As a general rule, rock and blues players tend to opt for heavier plectrums, and so if your pick weighs in at less than, say, .77mm thick, then it's almost definitely too light.

It's all down to physics, when you think about it. If you were going to be hitting a metal guitar string and you wanted the sound produced to be at all dynamic, then it makes perfect sense that the thing you'd be using to hit the string has got to be quite stable, or the pick itself would absorb most of the impact. A lighter pick might be fine for strumming chords gently on an acoustic guitar, but it's practically no good at all for good, old-fashioned, down-home blues.

Seeing as a plectrum is probably one of the cheapest bits of gear you're ever going to buy, you're not going to think it's unreasonable of me to suggest that you invest in, say, half a dozen of them at once, all of a different weights, thicknesses and sizes, and experiment.

You're bound to come up with one that suits your style of playing, but my advice is still to opt for one which is heavier than you think you'll eventually need. Don't go mad, of course; they make plectrums up to about 3mm in thickness, and this might prove a mite unwieldy – these have been dubbed as being 'jazz plectrums', where you're expected to be playing on seriously heavy-gauge strings most of the time. Tape-wound strings in particular are known for being unresponsive and in need of as hard a clout as is humanly possible, and a plectrum with a thickness of 3mm is ideal for this.

Check Your String Gauge

It might also be wise to reconsider the gauge of string on your guitar. In general, it's best to go for a gauge that is as heavy as you can stand. By default, most electric guitars come strung with a set of .009s, but a quick survey of blues players reveals that a set of .010s is far more in order.

There are even players they will opt for extremely heavy gauges of strings on their guitars: Stevie Ray Vaughan, for instance, used to use a top string that measured in at .013" or .014" and had the calluses to prove it! Of course, it's true that Stevie Ray used to compensate for this heavy gauge of string by tuning his guitar down to E♭, which would have made a difference in string tension, but all the same, his strings, like his playing, were still seriously heavy business.

Once again, guitar strings don't exactly cost a fortune, and so you can afford to experiment a little in this area, too. I would advise that you look at buying a set of strings one gauge up from the ones you are using now and just see if you can be comfortable with them. Tell yourself that string bending is going to feel different, even a little harder, but the results in terms of tone might well make this worth the investment.

Why the improvement in tone? It's back to the physics book once again: the more metal you have vibrating in the pick-up's magnetic field, the more powerful the signal for the amplifier to chew on, and this will result in a more accurate reading of the string's overall tone, taking into account things like vibrato and so on.

One word of caution here, though: if you have a guitar with a tremolo unit on – like the Fender Stratocaster, for instance – be prepared to have to make adjustments in order to compensate for the increase in string tension. Although this can be anything from a bother to a real pain, depending upon your skills with a screwdriver and your patience levels, it's still worth the effort if the overall effect is an improvement in tone.

Right-Hand Techniques

Now you've got some idea about the different gauges of plectrum and string available to you and have made a commitment to experiment a little in both areas, we'll get back to the hard-and-fast matter of technique. First up – and arguably one of the most important duties for the right hand – is actually sounding the strings...

How we actually choose to sound the string is, of course, up to us, and no one has the right to dictate to you or me whether we should be using a plectrum, our fingers, thumb- or finger-picks or a combination of all of the above. I say this because I meet students all the time who have been told that it's practically an offence against society to use anything other than what their teacher recommends!

Quite frankly, imposing anything like this on a pupil is downright twaddle and the teachers responsible should all be locked in a dark place until they see sense. There's a huge difference between recommending a course of action and insisting that you know what's best for another musician.

So now I've got that little number off my chest, I'll go on to say that a great percentage of blues players today choose to use a plectrum. This, of course, wasn't always the case, as the guitar in general seems to have been fingerpicked by tradition at the start of the blues's long and industrious life.

The point here is that the choice is up to you: if you want to use a pick, fine; if you want to use your fingers – with or without finger- and thumb-picks – equally fine. I'm only here to act as a guide; you must decide which way around feels the more comfortable for your right hand. It's really a decision that only you can make.

If you're not sure and could use some advice on the matter, I'd advise you to have a bash at both methods – it won't be long before you find it easier one way around or the other. So let's take both methods of attacking the strings in turn.

Using A Pick/Alternate Picking

As I said, if we were able to take a head count, it would probably reveal that most blues players and guitarists in general choose to use a pick. It's pretty much the default option and has both advantages and disadvantages built in.

One definite advantage is that of dynamics. I mentioned the physics involved when I was talking about plectrum weight a couple of paragraphs ago, and one thing is for certain: a piece of plastic hitting a string will set up more of a dynamic than using soft flesh or even the odd fingernail.

One of the only complaints I hear from fingerstyle players is that they have to adjust their thinking where dynamics are concerned and wish sometimes that using fingers presented more attack than was available. The other thing they complain about is wearing out their fingernails, but we'll come to Fingerstylists' Universal Complaint Number Two in just a minute.

Of course, there are as many ways of using a plectrum as there are of swinging a cat. I've seen plenty of haphazard picking techniques actually work in some way or other, and so I'm not going to claim that the way of proceeding that I'm about to recommend should be taken as set in stone. You'll adopt and adapt to suit your eventual playing style, but it is my belief that you stand a much higher chance of attaining a good level of competency if you adopt alternate picking as your standard early on.

Alternate picking is a system whereby downstrokes and upstrokes of the plectrum are strictly alternated, meaning that the notes you play are alternately sounded using up- and then downstrokes of the pick. It's a good discipline to adopt and it will give your playing a uniformity of tone and dynamics if carried out efficiently. What's more, I believe that, if you spend a while becoming familiar with alternate picking, you can more easily adapt to other picking styles later on, because the basic work has already been established.

Alternate picking also has one very good side-effect, which is that you absorb a lot about left- and right-hand co-ordination on the side while you're learning it. Obviously both hands have got to work with each other, and a little alternate picking against the metronome is ideal for getting your engine tuned in this respect.

To begin with, we'll follow the now-established pattern of isolating the job of picking away from your day-to-day playing, bung it under the microscope and see if we can't build a better one, so to speak...

Have a look at the example below. It's a scale fragment that operates over two strings:

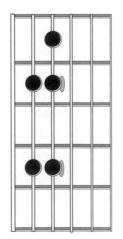

Start off by using a downstroke on the first note and follow it with an upstroke for the second, and so on. To begin with, play it dead slow – that's dead slow! Don't take for granted that this is something very simple that you can polish off in two or three minutes flat, because it's vital that you make sure that your picking is strictly alternate, and in order to do that you need time to take a close look.

If you own a metronome or drum machine (and, if you do, award yourself 100 bonus points, because they are both incredibly beneficial in the practice room and owning one or the other – or even both – shows terrific initiative on your part!), then set a beat of around 60–80 beats per minute and try to play one note per click. If this feels instantly really easy, maybe because you've been playing for ages and dealt with your picking way back in the nursery days, just take long enough to make sure that your picking really is alternate and then take the speed up a notch or two.

Just a couple of minutes a day doing this simple exercise is usually enough to establish alternate picking as a basis for everything you do – and it will also heighten your level of accuracy, too.

Naturally, picking using a plectrum isn't confined strictly to playing single lines or solos; occasionally, you'll be called on to play arpeggiated parts, and you can practise alternate picking here, too.

Take an ordinary C major chord down at the nut, like this one:

Play it across the strings from bass to treble and back again, using alternate picking all the time.

As before, start this exercise slow enough to allow you to take a close-up look at what's going on with your right hand and then speed it up gradually over a period of time.

Obviously, these exercises aren't exhaustive if your aim is to polish your picking skills to a shine, but they will certainly set you off in the right direction and allow you to build some solid foundations upon which later work can be carried out.

In practice, you'll find that playing actual pieces live or just jamming with friends calls for you to adjust your picking technique to suit, but at least you're going to have something solid to work on to begin with.

For example, you'll find that one of the major differences between a downstroke and an upstroke is the dynamic of the stroke itself. Obviously a downstroke is going to tend to be heavier than an upstroke – if only from the point of view that 'up' goes against gravity and doesn't have the weight of the hand behind it like 'down' does.

So, in order to take advantage of the greater thwack per pick stroke, you might want to play riff passages (blues is certainly rife with riff passages) using all downstrokes, instead of steering the alternate route.

Similarly, with solos, you can make more of a dynamic statement if several consecutive notes are carried out using downstrokes...

...but alternate picking will win hands-down for speed and fluency in the general run of things.

Whatever you do, don't allow yourself to become obsessed with picking and picking speed and spend an inordinate amount of time pursuing metronome speeds in the 180bpm range – as a blues guitarist, you're not really going to need this kind of speed. If you are fluent while playing sixteenth notes at a metronome speed of 120bpm, you should be able to handle most things.

Right-Hand Muting

As with left-hand muting earlier, this is an essential technique to master as it affects your overall sound, especially in the phrasing department. It also does a lot to clean things up and stop obtrusive open strings ringing when they shouldn't.

Muting became more and more necessary as amplifiers got louder and more powerful. It's interesting to compare the different levels of muting applied during the '60s, '70s and '80s, for instance.

During the early part of the '60s, muting was only light, owing to the fact that most players were still using relatively low-powered combos that didn't offer the same levels of sustain that the designer-hell hags from the '90s did. This has quite an effect on the actual authenticity of the sound from this era; basically, if you want to recreate an accurate '60s blues sound, you need to back off the gain on your amp and lessen the need for too much muting.

Take, as an example, the difference between Eric

Clapton's playing on the John Mayall 'Beano' album and the later live Cream albums. At Cream volume levels (Eric would often have two or three Marshall 100-watt stacks behind him on stage), the degree of muting heard in his playing actually changed his sound quite considerably.

If we then fast-forward to the 1980s, when higher and higher levels of saturation from pedigree valve amplifiers were sought to satisfy the needs of the post-Van Halen guitar players, muting had increased to the point at which some passages sound almost pizzicato (that means almost completely muted – and it's definitely my favourite word with two Zs in it, after *pizza* and *jazz*!).

What can we draw from all this? Well, basically, I think that you can't play '60s blues with '80s muting – and anyone who tries it is playing 'rock blues' and not the pure form. Call me prejudicial, but then take a listen to some rock blues and you'll see what I mean.

So, if we take a close look at right-hand muting, what do we find? Basically, you need to train the fleshy edge of your right palm (the bit you used to karate-chop your mates with when you were younger) to lay down on the strings in front of the bridge of the guitar.

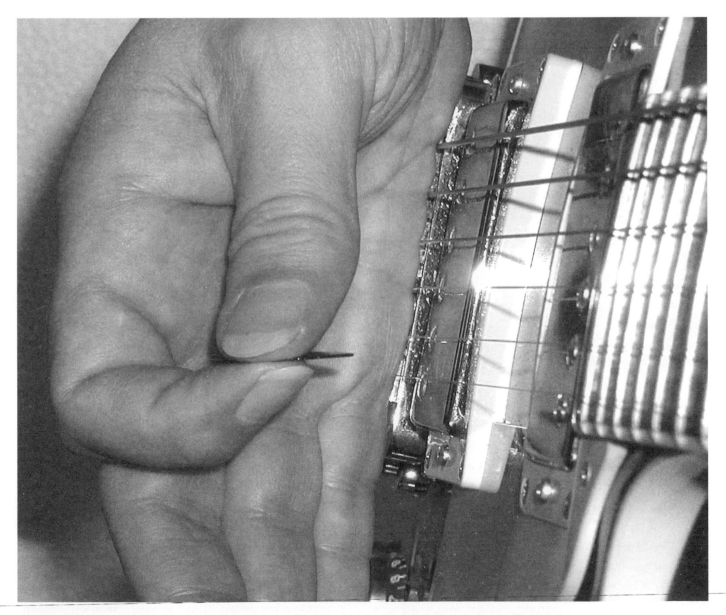

Right-hand muting position. The fleshy part of the palm lays down on the strings just before the bridge. Varying the pressure here will produce different degrees of muting (photo © Carol Farnworth 2003)

Next, work out what sort of range is available to you, in terms of 'mute power'. Obviously, one end of your range is leaving the strings completely unmuted and ringing open, while the other is with the strings fully muted so that all you end up with is a sort of musical

chunk sound when you hit the strings.

Now, given that these two parameters lie at either end of your muting capacity, you can explore what happens between them. Start off by playing a riff passage, like the one next:

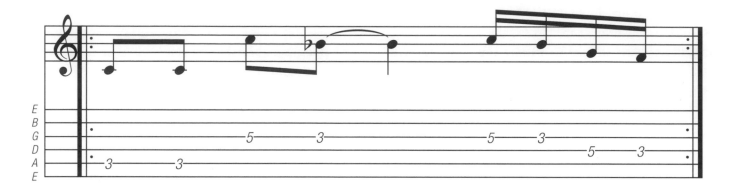

Now experiment with the sound of this particular riff using varying degrees of muting. The most important thing here is to listen to what sound you're producing – don't get carried away; you can relax and let off some steam later on in your practice routine. Just listen to what's going on and try to remember it. Then introduce it at different points in the things that you can already play to vary the effect a little.

Playing Fingerstyle

As I said earlier, I advise people to have a go at both plectrum and fingerstyle side by side for a while and form their own opinions as to which suits them best.

Personally, I tend to play fingerstyle quite a lot of the time, and the reason why I settled into it was purely because playing with a pick still felt awkward after I'd been playing for about 20 years, and I sort of got the message by then. It's different for all of us, but you won't be able to make the best possible choice unless you try things both ways around.

For a start, if you want to explore fingerstyle I'll warn you about a couple of things up front. For a start, metal strings tend to tear fingernails quicker than anything. Classical guitarists play with their nails, but they're dealing with nylon strings, which don't tend to do as much damage – but I do know a few classical players who are paranoid about their nails.

Various metal-string fingerstylists employ different remedies to beat the nail-chomping characteristics of their instruments. I know a few who use nail varnish to protect their nails, and it's not the extreme measure it might seem to be. After all, these guys play for a living, and so nail care is a priority – you can borrow a plectrum if you forget one but you can't borrow fingernails.

I'm lucky in that I was born with fingernails more like talons than your average nails, and I rarely have to worry about them in performance. But everybody is different in this respect – some people have fingernails that tear like paper while others, like me, have virtually Kryptonite-proof Supernails!

Of course, you might find yourself playing with the fleshy tips of your right-hand fingers, in which case the most you can expect is some discomfort during the initial callus-forming period (just like you experienced on your left hand), but after that you're virtually home free. The method you decide on – nail or flesh – will be sorted out for you as you continue to play.

We all go through several determining processes as our playing develops, the choices being made based on whatever feels more comfortable at the time. It's important to keep an open mind throughout these processes: my own playing has seen me adopting and abandoning different methods and techniques continually during the time I've been a guitarist.

It's something that doesn't necessarily stop – so remember to question yourself every so often, asking 'Does this really still work for me?', and you should be fine.

Fingerstyle Up Close

In much the same way that I said I've seen every kind of seemingly chaotic picking technique produce results, there are plenty of variations available to you as a fingerstylist. As you probably know by now, my recommended way through the maze of alternatives is to begin by steering a tried and trusted route and make whatever variations you need to along the way.

With this in mind, I'll take a few minutes to cover the basics of fingerstyle so that you can experiment and adapt them to suit.

As far as a discipline for using the fingers of the right hand to pluck the strings is concerned, we have to look no further than our classical counterparts, whose tradition of playing fingerstyle goes back

centuries. In other words, the techniques that they have adopted have had a chance to 'settle' into something that really works!

With classical guitar, the fingers of the right hand are identified via their Spanish names:

- thumb = *pulgar* (abbreviated to p);
- index = *indicio* (abbreviated to i);
- middle = *medio* (abbreviated to m);
- ring = *anular* (abbreviated to a).

In very general terms, your thumb – p – is your bass player, looking after the lower three strings. Meanwhile, the rest of the fingers look after the melody and harmony by being very approximately assigned a string each: i looks after the G string, m the B, and a the top E.

This is certainly the kind of formula you'd adopt for playing an arpeggiated C major chord, like the one shown below.

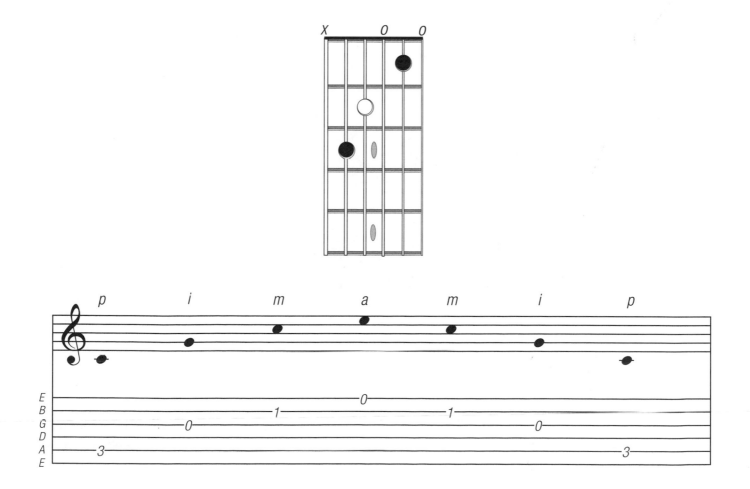

Hand position is reasonably critical here – mainly from the point of view that you need a position that doesn't restrict movement or cause tension in the right hand at all – and, on a very basic level, you just want the fingers to stay out of each other's way!

So, a guitarist's-eye view of a good all-round playing position would look something like the following photograph:

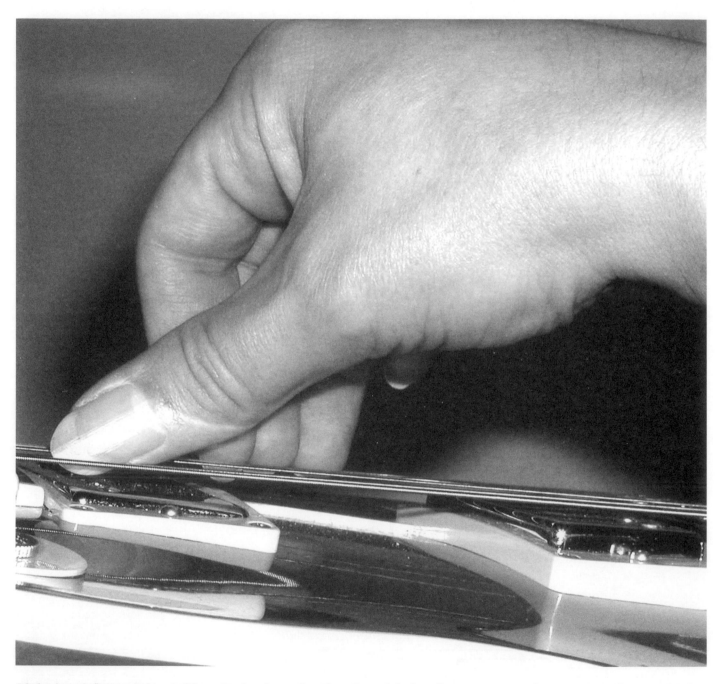

Right-hand fingerstyle position. Notice how the thumb and index finger seem to form an X to keep out of each other's way (photo © Carol Farnworth 2003)

As you can see, the thumb and index finger form something of an X. The only reason for this is so that they keep out of the way of each other when plucking: a simultaneous upstroke from the index finger and a downstroke from the thumb shouldn't result in a collision this way around.

In order to bring about a reasonable facility with the right hand, you have to adopt a practice schedule that contains plenty of exercises that will not only flex the fingers but give you a good degree of all-round digital independence at the same time.

For years I have been recommending a classical book by Mauro Giuliani called *Studies For Guitar* that concentrates on just this idea. Half of the book is dedicated to right-hand independence and is a grand workout, irrespective of style. The exercises keep things simple for the left hand by featuring the same two chords – C major and G7 – over and over, while the right-hand fingers go through an SAS-style assault course. What can I say? It works. Try it.

Some general rules for the right hand might include the following couple of points:

- Don't rest the right hand on the front of the guitar. To put it another way, don't try to anchor a finger or wrist to the top of the guitar, as this restricts movement in the hand and you'll definitely have trouble swapping from one style of guitar (ie flat top) to another (ie archtop). It's best to try and maintain a 'one size fits all' principle as far as possible;

- Try to keep the wrist in a straight line with the forearm. A humped wrist can encourage medical problems with the tendons which are not only painful but for which the only real cure is to stop playing and rest the arm for a long period of time. Best avoided, methinks!

Apart from that, almost anything goes. As I've said from the beginning, blues didn't come with a handbook; instrumental technique evolved along with the music itself, and as long as you take the attitude that your own technique might need the odd evolutionary review every so often, all should be well.

Guitar Tone

Let's face it, electric-guitar players very rarely use the control marked 'Tone' on their instruments, preferring instead to set up a single sound through the amplifier and use the Volume control to suit. But it's true to say

that the most important tonal variations aren't necessarily to be found here, in any case.

'When I'm playing, I fiddle around with the sound a lot, changing the tone, so at times that guitar will get full, at other times I back it off. It's just depending on how I feel at the time, really.' *Gary Moore*

On any guitar – it doesn't matter if it's electric or acoustic, nylon- or steel-strung – there's a wealth of tonal variation available just by adjusting your playing position slightly. It's a simple tool, and yet it's one that tends to be overlooked most of the time.

In order to explore the tonal capabilities of your guitar, compare the sound of a pickstroke near the bridge to one near the neck. You should notice that the pickstroke over the end of the fretboard sounds sweeter and more mellow than the one near the bridge. It's wise to establish these two parameters at least before working to produce the different natural tones available to you which lie between.

Varying the attack with either pick or fingers will have an effect on the sound you're making, too. Each guitar has a set of natural dynamics, and the way to examine these is simple, once again.

If you play acoustic guitar, establish the difference between loud and soft by experimenting with different weights of pick- or fingerstroke. Only when you know how loud or quiet an instrument can play can you begin to understand its true dynamic range.

This is another thing that is often left on the side by guitar students everywhere: many have no sense of dynamics in their playing at all and believe that the only influence over volume that they have is dependent on the instrument's Volume control – if it has one. Not true – before you make demands upon your guitar, make sure you know its range, both tonally and dynamically.

Guitar–Amplifier Interface

When you get to the stage when you're quite happy that your dynamic facility from a purely acoustic point of view is fully in hand, it's probably time to reconsider your guitar's relationship with its amplifier.

Many, many times I've heard students complain bitterly that their amplifier is obviously no good because they can't get a good sound from it, and should they try buying one that's twice the price/output to see if it improves matters? Invariably, my answer has been to take a good look at the controls on the front of the offending amplifier, because this is usually where the problem truly lies. For this reason, I very rarely appear at workshops with anything other than a cheap, low-powered practice amp in the hope that I'm demonstrating the fact that good tone comes from good technique, general awareness of such things like dynamics and so on, and definitely not how much your equipment cost!

The first thing I do is to turn down the Gain setting on the amplifier. For a recent '60s blues seminar I did in London, I had my Gain setting on less than 1 on the front panel and had all the push and tone I needed to demonstrate soloing techniques from the period fairly accurately.

The fact is that many guitar students rely too much on high gain settings because it means less work at the picking end of the guitar-playing operation. This kind of thinking represents free entry to the land of bad habits and should be avoided at all costs. I advise my students to practise acoustically most of the time, either on an acoustic guitar or an unplugged electric. This means that what you hear is what you get when you plug into an amp – you're doing the right amount of work for the amp to take over and produce the goods, in other words. Remember, too, that many guitarists in the classic blues era used to set up one basic sound on the amp and then adjust the guitar's Volume control to suit. If you experiment with this, you'll find that, with the guitar on 3–4 you've got a good, cleanish sound for chords. Turned up to around 7–8, you'll have a good crunch sound for riff accompaniment and so on, while full on should give you a good solo sound. This differs from guitar to guitar, but if you play around a bit, you should find something that works.

Next, I'd be inclined to make sure that your amplifier's pre-amp controls (Treble, Bass, Middle or whatever) are as flat as possible, meaning that, if there's a place where the treble or bass is not actually being boosted or reduced, that's the place you want to start. Very little adjustment should be necessary here – you don't want the bass or treble full up. If you do, there's something wrong!

Take care when setting your amp controls and always keep the sound you make with your guitar acoustically in mind when you do so and everything should be fine.

7 STYLE ANALYSIS

'I learned a lot of my stuff from the late Guitar Slim and some of the great guitar players and horn players and keyboard players.' Buddy Guy

If you cast your mind back to the chapter on blues melody, I mentioned that the subtle art of cherry picking – that process of extracting single licks, jackdaw-like, from other players' styles – is an extremely valuable aid when it comes to putting together a style of your own.

An extension of this would be to study the styles of various different players and to do a little bit of deconstructive analysis – literally seeing what makes them tick. This is another great way of harvesting ideas that you can then include in your own playing.

It's possible to learn something from just about everyone, latch on to signature licks and phrases and, in doing so, increase both your vocabulary and your versatility enormously.

I thought it would be a good idea to include here a sort of potted analysis of some of the more outstanding blues players as an illustration to how this sort of thing works.

The players I've chosen are:

- Muddy Waters;
- Mississippi Fred McDowell;
- Elmore James;
- Howlin' Wolf;
- John Lee Hooker.

Each player has the spotlight turned upon him in turn in a self-contained lesson, with the examples backed up on the CD. Study all of them, absorb as much as you can and then go and do the same sort of thing to other players of your own choice.

The key here is to continue your research – keep your curiosity stimulated to pick up new angles and views from the blues terrain.

Muddy Waters

Muddy Waters was born in Mississippi in 1915 and started to play guitar at around the age of 17, having picked up harmonica several years earlier.

Despite being hailed as the 'father of electric blues', Muddy actually spent many years playing acoustic guitar, including his first year in Chicago, way back in 1943. In those days, the electric guitar was simply a means to be heard over the general hubbub in the clubs and juke joints, and this was the main reason why Muddy managed to convince an uncle of his to get hold an electric guitar for him – he simply wanted to be heard!

Muddy used both thumb- and fingerpicks on acoustic guitar, moving on to thumbpick and fingers on electric – and this is partly responsible for his very rhythmic accompaniment style.

He used altered tunings fairly liberally during the early part of his career, employing a capo to implement key changes from song to song. In the examples on the CD, I've stuck to standard tuning in order to keep things as universally accessible as possible – and no capo, either.

Once you've picked up all the basic fingerpicking ideas presented here, though, please feel free to explore all of the different keys using a capo as it certainly adds a unique texture to some of the traditional blues repertoire.

When I was researching Muddy's style, I came across a few blues songs in some very strange keys – C♯ was one example – which means either that Muddy was using a capo to its fullest effect and choosing to play in unusual keys or that the actual tuning of his guitar was slightly off!

It's a thing to watch out for in early blues: soloists seemed to regard tuning as optional and, in many cases, close was close enough.

Influences

Muddy's primary influence was legendary bluesman Son House, although his style included at least a courteous nod of the head in Robert Johnson's direction, too. Remember, this was the young man who Alan Lomax found could faithfully recreate Johnson's repertoire when he first came across him during his Library of Congress mission!

On the accompanying CD example, I've recorded two verses of a simple 12-bar pattern in E, attempting to combine as many elements of Muddy's style as I could. Muddy wouldn't necessarily pack everything quite so tight, as his accompaniment style was more open and sparse. So, if you include all the ideas here during a full blues by spreading them out a bit, you should have got things just about right. Economy can speak volumes!

The first thing to notice is how the E chord is played in a D7 shape at the fourth fret, as opposed to the more familiar nut position. This was very much a part of the country-blues style of playing and it's certainly possible to see where Jimi Hendrix got the intro to 'Red House' from.

When the E7 chord resolves into the A7, there's a noticeable descent, which wouldn't have otherwise been presented had we been using more conventional chord voicings. This adds a lot of character and a spot of local colour to the proceedings straight away and is a perfect foil for the voice. For this reason – and others, of course – it's always worth experimenting with different chord voicings to hear the effects that they can have on the music.

Any fills that crop up will be taken from the E minor pentatonic scale with the flat fifth added and are used to break up the accompaniment.

○ = flat fifth

Other than that, there is quite a marked 4/4 going on in the bass.

Muddy not only used a thumb pick to accentuate the bass on his guitar, but he was also in the habit of slapping his hand against the strings to produce a similar rhythmic effect. I've put a certain amount of this on the recording on the CD, but not so much that it gets in the way of being able to decipher exactly what's going on.

Naturally, this rhythmic style of keeping the beat calls for the thumb to play a regular rhythm while the rest of the fingers pick against it, and this can cause some problems early on.

The best way to approach this particular technique is to practise on open strings: by taking the left hand out of the equation completely, it leaves you with more brain power to concentrate on what exactly is going on with the right-hand thumb and fingers. It also helps if you tap your foot in time, too. It might sound like a cliché, but it acts as a great pacer for what's going on with the fingers. I know of a couple of blues players who, when they go out on the road, take with them a special board which is placed on the stage, miked up and used for tapping their feet on just to push the music along.

Other than that, there are no huge technical challenges here – this kind of playing is more down to 'feel' in any case, and problem areas will iron themselves out over time. Practise getting things in time and sounding clean.

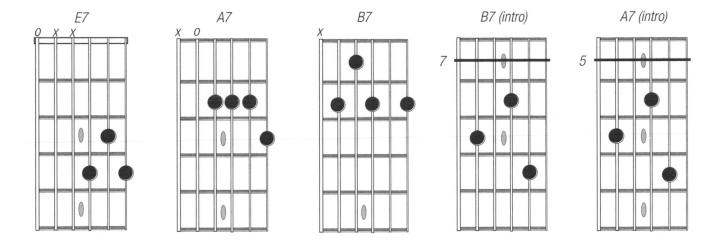

Let all chords ring into each other throughout

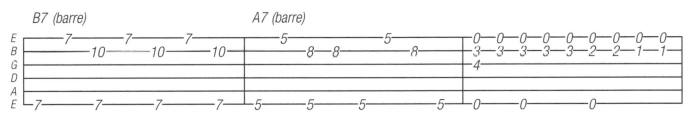

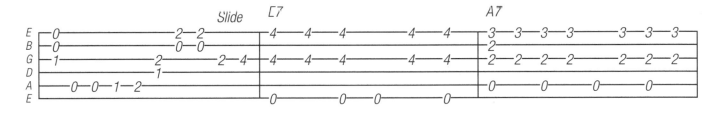

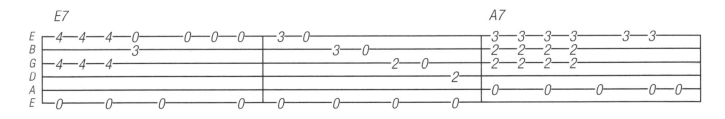

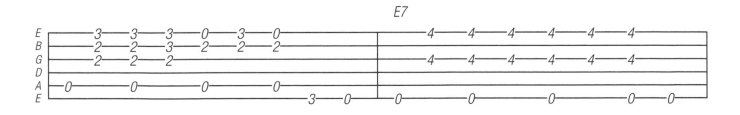

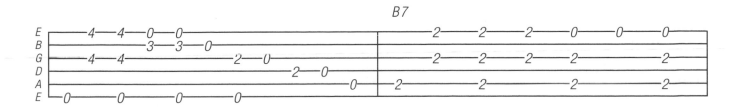

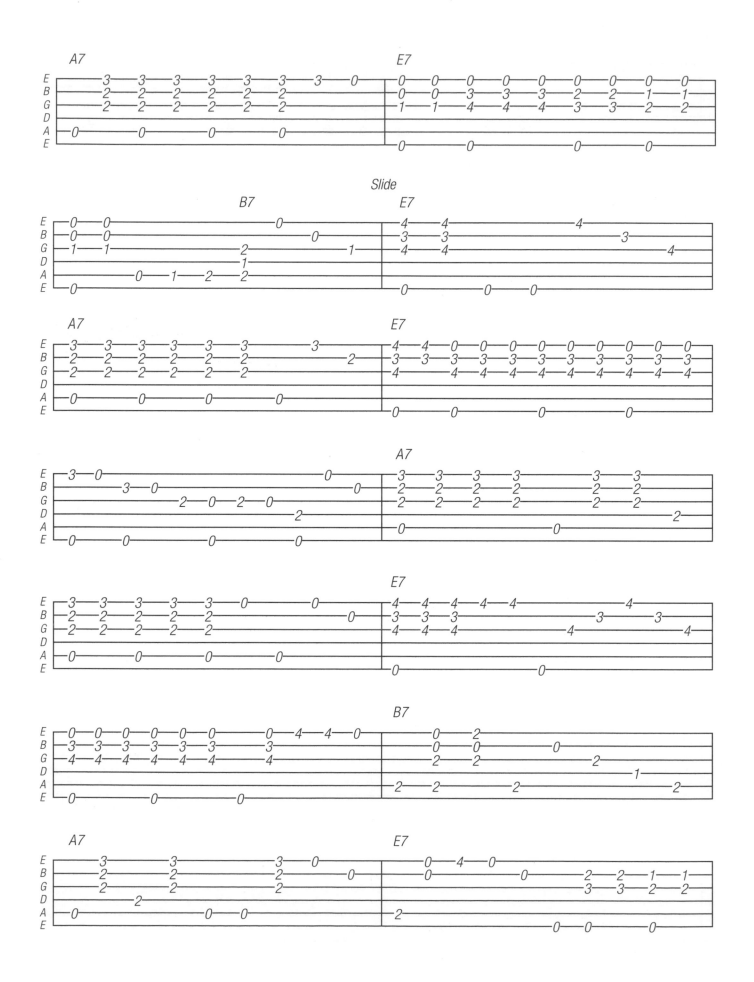

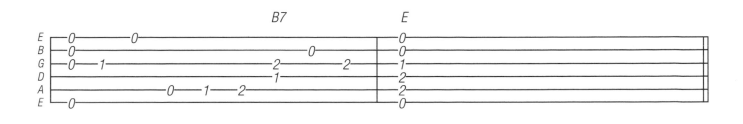

Further Listening

There's a lot of Muddy's material around, although most of it displays his electric playing, 'tis true. The real seminal stuff is to be found on *The Complete Plantation Recordings*, for which Muddy borrowed an acoustic guitar and created history. There is a fine album called *Muddy Waters And Friends* which has some good acoustic playing on it from both Muddy and Otis Spann, and I'm sure if you delve deep into historical blues reissues, you'll find more!

Mississippi Fred McDowell

Mississippi Fred McDowell is quoted as saying, 'I do not play no rock 'n' roll,' and yet his influence on the modern purveyors of the blues's rockier side is considerable. He's credited with some fine blues standards, including 'Louise', 'Jesus Is On The Mainline', 'Kokomo Me Baby' and many more.

Contemporary artists like Bonnie Raitt credit Fred McDowell as a significant influence on their styles, Bonnie featuring a tribute to the man in her live show under the heading 'Kokomo Medley'.

Funnily enough, in view of his nickname, Mississippi Fred was actually born in Rossville, Tennessee, moving to Mississippi only later, in 1940. Of this curious fact, Fred says, 'It don't make any difference, and I seem like I'm at home there whenever I'm in Mississippi.'

One of the major things that Fred brought to guitar playing was his sense of rhythm. At the time, blues might have been veering towards the shuffle rhythm that you hear in every blues jam today, but Fred's style

was upbeat, almost a straight eighth-note rhythm, as opposed to the dotted-eighth-note style adopted by many who have been lured by the 12-bar blues' charms.

So the first thing to do is to establish this particular rhythm in the fingers of the right hand. I've recorded an example on the CD of how the rhythm should sound on a basic E major chord. The main point of focus here is the thumb: you're playing the main beats of the bar with this digit, and so it's here that you must set up the driving rhythm around which everything else will be built. Good, solid downstrokes with the thumb on the bass strings of the guitar will make everything else you do sound tight and solid, and so it's worth spending a little time getting this basic element completely right.

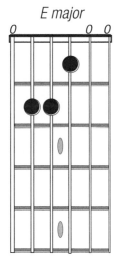

E major

Try the basic rhythm on a static E major chord. The thumb looks after the bass and the fingers play the top strings on the offbeat

Fingers

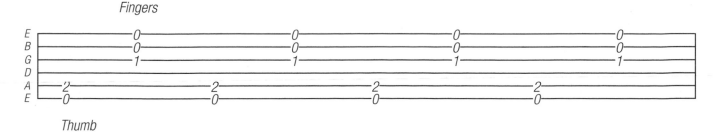

Thumb

I would advise you to practise with a metronome. There really isn't a better way of honing your rhythm playing. It's a thing I still do to this day – just put the metronome on, set up a rhythm on the guitar and then try to vary the rhythm around the beat.

In any case, you'll need to start with a fairly slow speed on the metronome at first – about 70–90 beats per minute ought to do the trick. Make sure that your thumb plays in perfect sync with the click. Once you're sure that everything's running like clockwork, try adding the offbeat with your fingers. By this I mean that, if you're playing 1–2–3–4 with your thumb, you add the eighth notes with your fingers so that you're playing 1-and-2-and-3-and-4-and between the thumb and the fingers.

This is the engine that drives this particular rhythm along, and I would strongly advise against going any further until this part has been mastered and you can play it every time fluently, cleanly and without dribbling, if at all possible...

Once the rhythm is up and running, take a look at the little motif we're going to superimpose over the top of it. We're using the open strings to help us out here, but you're going to be adding this little motif to the E, A and B7 chords, and so you've got to be sure that your fingers really know it thoroughly before proceeding further. As a practice routine, try putting the motif over the E chord to begin with. Once you've got this straight, the other two chords should fall naturally into place.

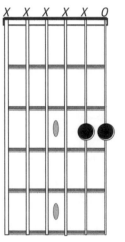

As for an exact right-hand fingering, all I can tell you is that, when I recorded the demo for the CD, I used my thumb for the bass, my index finger for the offbeat and my middle and ring fingers for the blues motif. You may find yourself working out another way of doing it, and if that works, fine.

Keep checking your timing with a metronome – while I realise that the blues is not always run to military disciplines where timing is concerned (especially unaccompanied acoustic blues), you'll find that it's actually easier to take liberties with your timing when it's been drilled to perfection first.

Despite the fact that this lesson sounds fairly simple on the CD, it's a lot harder than it sounds, and so remember to take things slowly and bring everything up to tempo gradually.

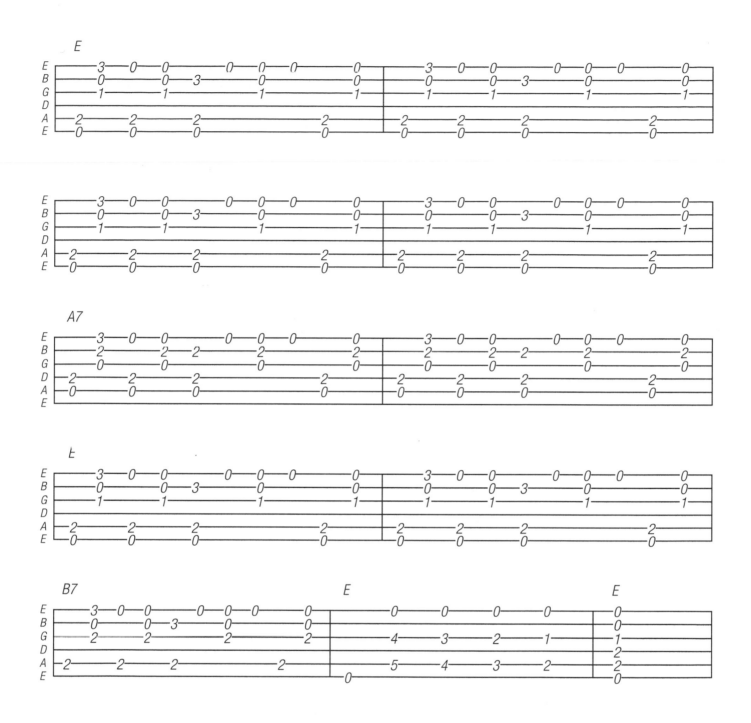

Further Listening

Take a listen to Bonnie Raitt's 'Kokomo Medley' (there's an excellent version on the *Road Tested* CD and live DVD) for a modern interpretation of what Mississippi Fred McDowell has brought to the blues. You should also try to find some of the man's work; there are a few compilations around featuring a good selection of tracks.

Elmore James

Elmore James was probably best known for his electric slide playing, and we're not exactly looking at slide here, but we can learn a little from everyone, irrespective of style or technique, so listen up!

Elmore James was born in Richland, north of Jackson, Mississippi, in January 1918 and learned guitar from listening to Robert Johnson – or so the story goes. It's alleged, too, that he played with Johnson on occasion at some of the infamous juke joints in the Delta region.

A religious man, James often played guitar in church and was seemingly a reluctant blues hero. His recording of 'Dust My Broom' was a hit, and that led him on to doing tours and playing dates in the north of the USA, but he was always eager to return home.

His slide style and singing voice had all the agonised qualities of Robert Johnson, and he often played with Sonny Boy Williamson – another legend in his own right.

James got a job as a radio DJ and almost regarded playing guitar as his second job, but eventually he joined the blues-musician migration north and went to live in Chicago, where he apparently didn't like the cold, as it upset his asthma. He died in 1963.

When I first heard Elmore James, probably as a teenager, I was sure he was singing, 'I woke up this morning, believe I'll dust my room,' and I thought, 'You can't have a blues about doing housework, surely?' Then, later on, I discovered the real lyric. I'm not exactly sure what 'dust my broom' alludes to, but I don't think it's anything as innocent as doing a bit of dusting...

As an example of Elmore James's style, I've constructed a blues in E that uses a guitar motif very similar in style to that of the intro to 'Dust My Broom'. Although the original was played using a bottleneck, we can adapt it and turn it into a nice intro on acoustic guitar or electric, too, without a lot of effort.

The first thing to look at is the chord employed for the intro. It's really a snippet of an E major chord played at the 12th fret.

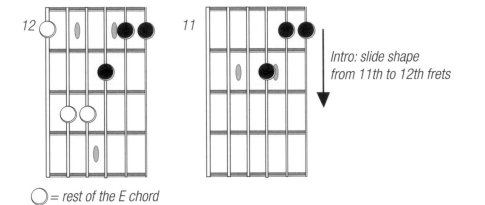

Intro: slide shape from 11th to 12th frets

◯ = rest of the E chord

You might have to work on the technique I've used for imitating the slide, but don't worry – it's not as hard as it sounds. It's just a question of taking a firm hold on the chord and sliding it from fret 11 to fret 12 in rhythm. The rhythm concerned is triplets, which you count by taking a three-syllable word of your choice and saying it along in time. I recommend the word *evenly*, because that's how a triplet should be played. If you want to take a more mathematical stance, however, try merely counting '1–2–3, 1–2–3' along as you play.

The other two chords in the blues are regular barre chords for A7 and B7, with the E slide motif returning when the arrangement turns around to E once again.

Finally, there's the familiar blues turnaround on E at the end to finish off the verse.

If you're going to play this example fingerstyle (which is really what it was designed for, although electric players will be able to adapt it for playing with a pick), you should familiarise yourself with the standard right-hand fingerstyle convention of using the thumb to look after the three bass strings while the index, middle and ring fingers see to the treble side of the action.

Blues fingerstyle wasn't nearly as precise as some of the fingerpicking you hear today. It was less organised and more haphazard, and so I'm inviting you to loosen up a bit here.

Much of the attack on the strings was quite passionate, though, and often quite muted, too, so pay special attention to your dynamics and muting technique for a more realistic approach.

Muting may feel unnatural at first, but even classical guitarists have to learn the technique of placing the fleshy side of the right hand palm down on the strings until they achieve pizzicato – that's the

classy name for muting, to you and me. Ideally, you should still be able to hear the note, but most of the sustain or 'ringing on' is cut short. If this technique continues to trouble you, try practising it for a couple of minutes a day in isolation from any piece you might be learning. Experiment with different pressures on the strings until you hear something that clicks as being right.

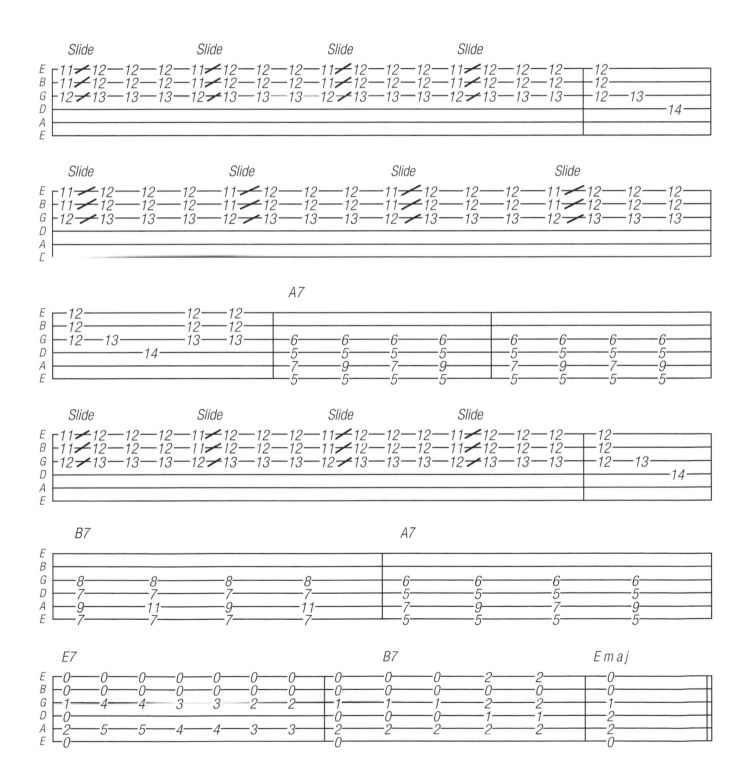

Further Listening

Obviously, anything by Elmore James, especially his version of 'It Hurts Me Too'. Take note of how Eric Clapton's version is virtually a carbon copy of the original (I'm sure this was a deliberate homage on EC's part – I'm not accusing 'imself of anything tacky). Getting hold of any of the Delta blues compilations (as advised elsewhere in this book) would be a good idea to give yourself a cross-section of the different styles on offer, too. Don't limit yourself to listening to guitarists, though; you can pick up a lot from listening to the harp players and singers of the era, too.

Howlin' Wolf

Chester Burnett (the Wolfman's real name) was born in Aberdeen in 1910. (That's Aberdeen, Mississippi, incidentally, although it would be amusing to fantasise about what blues would have sounded like if it had originated in the Scottish Highlands...) It was said that he took lessons from Charley Patton, who is today generally acknowledged as being the founding father of modern blues. According to legend, Chester Burnett was transformed into Howlin' Wolf by Jimmie Rodgers, who nicknamed the singer after hearing his rough, throaty vocal style.

It's true to say that Wolf isn't particularly remembered for his guitar playing, although he was often seen with an acoustic guitar in his hands. It was more his singing voice and writing ability that guaranteed him blues immortality. Songs like 'Who's Been Talking' (recorded by Robert Cray), 'Commit A Crime' (recorded by Stevie Ray Vaughan), 'Killing Floor' (recorded by Led Zeppelin) and 'Louise' (recorded by just about everyone) have permeated the blues repertoire and are staples of blues set lists across the planet.

The guitarist most associated with Howlin' Wolf was Hubert Sumlin, and this is the man from whom we can gain some accompaniment ideas that transfer readily to acoustic fingerstyle. Just out of interest, Clapton is on record as saying that Sumlin had one of the weirdest styles he'd ever heard.

To begin with, let's consider a few facts. Most of the post-World War II electric players learnt their stuff on acoustic guitar, so if ever you're in the position of playing blues detective and are successful in tracking down some of the early blues recordings, you'll find out how things have evolved. It was much later on that blues-guitar solos took centre stage; back in the good old days, it was more likely you'd find emphasis placed on vocals, harmonica and piano – in that order. In 'city blues', the guitar was more often than not considered a semi-rhythm instrument, concentrating on fills and accompanying riffs more than on any fiery fretboard gymnastics.

A very rich source of accompaniment ideas can be found down near the guitar nut. Here, once again, is the 'open E' blues scale:

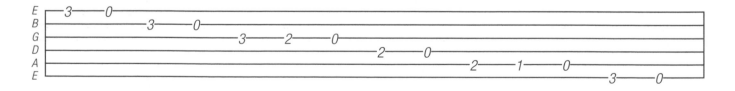

If you remember, it's basically the minor pentatonic scale with an added flat fifth, but it was responsible for some memorable musical moments during the heyday of Chicago blues. If you wrap it around an E7 chord, you'll find loads of things that sound very familiar indeed.

One thing about the open-position blues scale, though: you can't bend the third on the G because it's an open string. As you know, part of what gives the blues its distinctive timbre is the slightly sharp third, which guitarists usually compensate for by bending the string concerned.

As this isn't possible in the open position, it was quite common for guitarists of the period to employ a trill instead – a trick they probably learned from hearing piano players. The fretboard diagram (right) and the tab (below) illustrate how this is done.

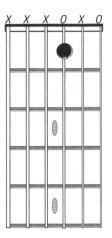

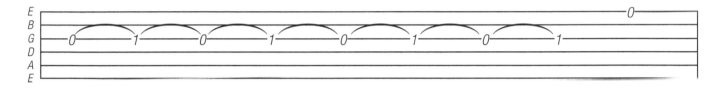

The above example demonstrates how you can include this vital blues sound in your playing. It takes a bit of co-ordination, but nothing that a bit of earnest practice can't buff to a shine.

Next is an accompaniment device that was used wholesale by the Wolf and Muddy Waters. You'll hear similar parts in songs like 'Little Red Rooster', 'I'm A Man', 'Hootchie Coochie Man' and dozens more.

Basically, the idea comprises a rapid shift between A and E chords, topped off with a high E on the top string, 12th fret. I've heard this played with and without slide, and it's about as authentic to the blues as Mississippi mud, so it's definitely something that you should consider adding to your repertoire without delay.

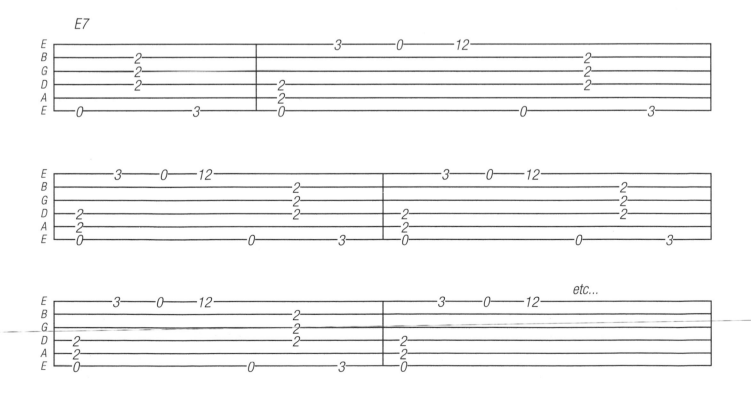

The whole thing relies on your ability to bend the top E string at the third fret before accurately targeting the 12th fret. You might have a few near misses, but once again it's nothing that practice shouldn't be able to sort out for you. Just take things slowly to begin with, and remember to keep a rhythm going somehow, just to fuse everything together. Even tapping your foot (like John Lee Hooker) can add pace to this particular rhythm part.

Further Listening

There are plenty of 'best of'-type recordings and other retrospectives available that demonstrate the Wolf's inimitable style. I'd recommend, too, that you track down some of the covers of his songs – like Zeppelin's version of 'Killing Floor', for instance. If you want a truly memorable listening experience, however, look no further than an album called *The London Sessions*. For this recording, Wolf came over to London to record with a band comprising some of London's elite young bluesmen, including Bill Wyman on bass, Stevie Winwood on keyboards, Charlie Watts on drums and Eric Clapton on guitar.

John Lee Hooker

Listen to any recording by John Lee Hooker and you'll hear the blues made real – but it's not done via any technical prowess, it's pure heartfelt emotion, and this is always a thing to remember when you're in the position of performing a blues song.

To round off this section on blues analysis, I've reproduced here an interview I conducted with John Lee Hooker shortly before he died. At the time, John Lee was 81 and still performing – and it was possibly one of the most difficult interviews I did! John Lee is not a man of many words, you see, and he often answered me with a well-chosen monosyllable where others – arguably a lot less great than he – would have chuntered on for ages.

I've still got a lot of affection for the man, though, and this interview sticks in my mind as being one of the most rewarding I've done. I felt that I had really come into contact with someone who had a direct link back to the time of the Delta heyday and that I was reaching out and touching the past by talking to him.

In any case, it's an interview that I'm proud to share, a conversation with one of the greatest blues musicians of his generation.

The Boogie Man: John Lee Hooker

John Lee Hooker doesn't talk; he growls. Speaking to him, you can see where the unique vocal delivery comes from – it's an intrinsic part of the man himself.

'Well, thank you,' he rumbles when I congratulate him on the release of his new album, *The Best Of Friends*, which celebrates his work from the last ten years. This period in his career has seen the legendary bluesman team up with luminaries from the rock and blues world, the resulting albums representing a massive upturn in John Lee's fortunes.

John Lee Hooker was born in Clarksdale, Mississippi, on 22 August 1917 and first picked a guitar up during his early teens. His stepfather, William Moore, was his first tutor on the instrument.

'I started playing when I was a kid, about 12 or 13. I was living with my stepfather and my mother, and it was my stepfather who taught me how to play. He gave me a guitar called a Stella. The stuff I'm playing now, that's his style.

'Then, when I was 14 or 15, I left home. I just took off, y'know? I didn't want to stay in the South and work on the farm; I figured there had to be a better way in the world and I headed north. Then, when I recorded "Boogie Chillun'", I got a hit on it.'

Did he play gigs in the South?

'No – I wasn't making records then. I didn't start making records until I got to Detroit.'

He made the move north during World War II and started to work on the automobile assembly lines. What sort of venues was he playing in those days?

'Oh, theatres and small nightclubs... I was playing the blues, I guess, same as I'm playing now. I've just updated that same thing.'

Who were John Lee's influences on the guitar around that time?

'Eddie Kirkland – you heard of him? Him and me, we played together for many years an' he learned from me and I learned from him.'

Records like 'Dimples', 'I Love You Honey' and 'I'm Ready' came out over the '50s and '60s, but John Lee's career really kicked into Grammy-laden overdrive after the release of the album *The Healer* in 1989. How the album came about in the first place had a lot to do with the collection of celebrity admirers John had collected around him up to that point. The list of willing collaborators was a long one, but the one man who was to implement in the sound, style and direction of *The Healer* album was Carlos Santana.

'I was living in California, the same city I'm living in now, and he used to come on my gigs all the time. Sometimes we'd be on the same gigs, his band and my band, we'd be on the same show. The first time I heard him, he was on one of my shows and I listened to him and got talking to him. We decided we wanted to do something together, so we did it and it turned out good.'

'Good' is probably an understatement – the album's title track won John a Grammy and a follow-up album became almost inevitable.

Another man who took a very active role in bringing John Lee to the world stage was Van Morrison.

'I met Van Morrison in Europe. He loved my style and he really can sing, so we did some things together. He's a good man.'

Other song partners who were originally long-term fans include Bonnie Raitt…

'She used to come to my shows all the time. She used to love the song 'In The Mood'. I met her and we got talking and she was really, really big at the time. When we came to record together, I asked her which song she wanted to do, and she wanted to do 'In The Mood' – that was the one thing she wanted, and she's a really good girl and I think she did justice to the song.'

Ry Cooder has shown up on a couple of John Lee's albums as both guitar player and producer.

'We just bumped into each other at gigs. My agent put us together to record and he produced me. He's a good man, a good guitarist – good all round.'

It is said that John Lee met Robert Cray after hearing Cray's *Bad Influence* album. Hook invited Cray to open for him on tour and the two are now firm friends.

'He's a very nice young man. I met him when he was living in Portland and he was playing small clubs. We recorded together – I like him a lot.'

John Lee has worked with a whole host of superstars during the last ten years. Has he a favourite?

'It's pretty hard to say. I worked with them all and I love them all and all of them are really nice people and good to work with.'

The new album is a compilation of some of the best of John Lee's collaborations during the last ten years, including a couple of new tracks, the most notable of these, perhaps, being a re-reading of Hooker's original hit, 'Boogie Chillun'', with Eric Clapton lending his considerable weight to the proceedings. Was this the first time the two had met?

'No, we've jammed in England. He's a great guitar player and a great person. I'm looking forward to seeing him again. I'm always glad to see him.'

'Boogie Chillun'' probably sums up everything good about the blues. On the original, there's just John Lee with his guitar, stomping foot and sub-bass vocals. The famous 'Last night I was laying down…' lyric has even turned up in live performances by Led Zeppelin. The song's influence has obviously burrowed deep and embedded itself in modern rock.

It's 50 years on from the original recording of 'Boogie Chillun'', but apparently Hook is not into the romance of the song's golden anniversary. When reminded of the special occasion, he merely remarks, 'Yeah, whatever.' This will be about the third time that he has recorded the song…

'Yeah, I've recorded it two or three times…'

The new version calls on the services of Jim Keltner on drums, Little Feat's Bill Payne on keyboards and, of course, Eric Clapton on guitar. How does John think the new version holds up?

'I think it's very nice. It sounds pretty good to me. We used more people and more instruments on it and it's got more kick to it.'

Talking of instruments, what sort of guitars is John Lee using at the moment?

'I use Gibsons or Epiphones.'

What sort of amplifier does John favour now?

'Fender Bassman and Rhythm King – I use both.'

One of the major characteristics of Hooker's style is his rhythm style on guitar. It seems that his thumb keeps a four-to-the-bar bassline going while his fingers sound the top strings with an upstroke. As a guitar style, it's quite unique, but where did it come from?

'My stepfather. He just taught me his style, a sort of rhythm-and-lead style. It's a strange style...'

During his early years, John Lee preferred to play solo rather than with a band...

'I played solo. I like playing by myself. I can get more into it.'

That, of course, has changed now...

'Oh, it's changed a lot.'

When asked who he listens to these days. There is a long, reflective silence.

'I used to play Albert King and Albert Collins...but now?' He thinks for a few more moments. 'Most of them are gone...' he says wistfully.

It has to be said that many bluesman would have hung up their hats and retired long ago, but at 81 there are as yet no signs of Hooker's career slowing down. What keeps him going?

'I'd like to know that myself... Sometimes I wonder what keeps me going, but I do just keep on going. And I love it – I figure it must be God or whatever, y'know?'

When I ask him if he intends ever to retire, his answer contradicts itself...

'Oh yeah. Pretty soon. Well, I'll probably keep playing, but not as much. I can't keep going on forever, but I'll play what I can for as long as I can – ya just gotta hang in there.'

Selected Discography

The Folk Blues of John Lee Hooker (Riverside 1959)
Live at the Cafe Au Go-Go (Bluesway 1967)
Urban Blues (Bluesway 1968)
Simply The Truth (Bluesway 1969)
The Healer (Virgin 1989)
Mr Lucky (Virgin 1991)
Jealous (Virgin 1996)

Look out for various compilations of early material such as *Hobo Blues* (Blues Encore), which features hits like 'Boogie Chillun'' and 'Dimples'.

8 SURVIVAL TIPS FOR PLAYING LIVE

'We're not trying to lay down something that's totally precise where the guitar solo has to be exactly this or the bass line has to be exactly that. That's the advantage we have of playing together as a band all the time; the song is there, the backbone is there – now it's time to have fun with it.' *Robert Cray*

When I go out to play a gig, there are things I never leave behind. For instance, over the years I've learned (mainly from experience, it has to be said) some important lessons. One of the most important is Murphy's Law...

Whoever Mr Murphy was, his law is certainly an invaluable reminder to us of the frailty of all things, because it states, 'If something can go wrong, it probably will...'

So, trying to beat Murphy's Law has become something of a life's mission for many musicians who acknowledge that you can't be prepared for everything, but you can at least cater for the obvious.

Carrying Spares

First of all, I would recommend everyone to carry with them a tool kit comprising a custom set of tools you need to make 'roadside repairs' to your instrument and amplifier whilst they are away from home. This needn't be something of the size you'd need if you were called out to service a jumbo jet; I manage to get everything I need in a soft camera case which measures about 7.5" x 3.5" and fits discreetly into the bag I keep leads and other guitar-related junk in, or, if I'm really travelling light, into my guitar case.

Inside, I have the following...

Spare Strings

I've met people who claim that they never break strings on stage, but don't think that it will never happen to you. Be prepared and don't leave home without a spare set of your favourite gauge of strings on board.

String Winder

This little device is one of the wonders of the nuclear age and can save you a lot of time during regular string changes but is invaluable in pit-stop string-change situations, too. It's a little mechanical doodad that fits over your tuning keys and, thanks to the wonders of mechanics, speeds up the rate at which you can wind and unwind strings. They're sold everywhere you go, they're cheap and you'll love me after a single string change for suggesting that you buy one. The deluxe version is motorised and used by professional guitar techs, who spend a good part of their daily routine changing strings.

Pliers

Yes, pliers, preferably the kind that can double as a string cutter. (Otherwise you might want to buy one of those, too – just make sure that you buy one that will cut piano wire and not just soft copper.) If I had a Euro for every time I've been asked if I had any pliers on me (usually by drummers), I would be listed on the stock exchange.

Screwdrivers

You don't need a whole set, just the ones you need to change fuses or make any emergency adjustments to other equipment you keep with you on the road.

Allan Keys

These are becoming less and less necessary on the road because the fashion for locking nuts and Floyd Rose-type tremolo units has diminished.

Spare Fuses

It's not only spare mains fuses you'll find going at the least convenient moment; amplifiers have fuses, too, and it's up to you to find out exactly what type and rating they are. It will cost you only a few pence to prevent red-faced silent running on stage. Trust me, I learned this one from experience...

Spare Batteries

If you use floor-mounted stomp-box effects, you'll need to carry spare batteries. It's the easiest thing in the world to think that a battery is going to last for one more gig, but they never go at a time that's convenient for you, so act like a boy scout and be prepared!

Luxuries

I used to carry a scalpel for stripping wires and I once knew a bass player who carried a soldering iron, but, like I say, you can't carry everything!

Guitar Tuners

However eclectic you are in the practice room (ie you might use a tuning fork and tune by ear), you can't afford to be without an electronic tuner out on the road. It's a question of speed and accuracy – both vital elements of a neat and tidy performance.

Tuners these days come in all shapes and sizes, and the ones that you merely plug in and tune your little heart out are fine for live use. You're quite likely to find that you can plug your tuner 'in line' with the rest of your gear so that it's always on during a performance. (Some effects pedals have auxiliary 'tuner outs' which allow this.) Keep it somewhere in view and you can even tune during a song if something untoward starts happening.

Remember that, no matter how in tune you are when you walk out there, things like humidity and (especially) heat caused by stage lights can throw your tuning out by a few cents with no trouble at all. I once had the embarrassing experience of picking up a guitar I used for only one number (a Telecaster tuned to open G for 'Brown Sugar') and I was halfway through the intro before I realised that the whole guitar was about a quarter of a tone flat. Just enough to make me sound like a total prat...

The tuner I use now is an Intellitouch, which clips onto your headstock in a very unobtrusive way and is always there for discreet tuning between songs.

Quality Leads

This is another thing that you simply cannot afford to buy cheap. I'm afraid it's a simple fact of life that cheap leads crackle and generally compromise your guitar sound. They also break easily and are generally the work of the Devil! Buying good-quality leads is a simple way of ensuring a relatively stress-free stage experience and a good sound. Just remember that Murphy's Law can be at work in this area, too, and take a spare just in case...

Spare Picks

It's the cheapest piece of kit you'll ever buy to satisfy your guitar-playing habit, but you'll find that you actually need more than you think. The fact is, picks fall out of sweaty hands, and it's far easier to reach for a new one than it is to get down on your knees and search a dimly lit pub floor.

Avoid clear picks, too. See-through picks might look nice and gimmicky, but, if you drop one, it's lost. A few years ago, someone came out with the idea of luminous picks, telling us that we needed never scramble about in the dark looking for a pick again, but to be honest, they didn't work; a plectrum would have to be practically radioactive to show up under normal gig conditions.

Road Map

This is very sound investment for anyone is looking at doing gigs, even if you think that you're staying local. I've been in so many situations where directions to small, out-of-the-way pubs only a few miles from where I live have been so inaccurate that I almost didn't make the gig. It's a very good idea to keep a contact telephone or mobile number for someone at the place you're playing with you, as well (see below).

Torch

Once again, a torch is the sort of thing you think you'll only ever need on a gig if your car breaks down, but you'd be surprised how many times I've had to set my gear up in very poor lighting conditions. Often, too, gear manufacturers don't help you out by putting important words like *input* or *output* in microscopic print on the back of their equipment in unhelpful colour combinations like blue on black. A mini torch like a MagLite (no self-respecting roadie is ever seen without one) will help out here in making sure that all your inputs and outputs are properly sorted.

Gloves

It might sound like something your mother would tell you, but a good pair of warm gloves are essential out there in winter gig land. Your hands have a lot of technical work to do when you start playing and they hate a cold start, so keep 'em warm at all costs.

In all weathers, a good pair of thickish leather gloves will help protect your hands from any ruinous run-ins with gear while you're loading and unloading, too. Playing with grazed knuckles is not a pleasant experience, let me assure you!

Painkillers

This was another lesson I learnt from bitter experience. Playing a gig on a hot Sunday in July, I arrived with the mother of all headaches and no one in the band had any Aspirin or Paracetamol to tame this pumping beast that had taken up residence behind my eyes, so I played the whole gig in horrible discomfort (stage lights can be particularly cruel under these circumstances) for the want of a cheap packet of instant relief.

Guitar Case

It has to be said that a good guitar case or sturdy gig bag both represent the cheapest form of insurance you can buy. Guitar cases might not be cheap, but they're not as expensive as replacing a treasured instrument.

I've heard so many would-be horror stories from friends in which cases have offered the protection necessary to avoid a dear one from getting hurt, if you see what I mean. I've also heard some stories in which cases would have prevented some nasty accidents, too – an old friend of mine had his guitar neck snapped in two because it was left unattended and uncased. Makes you weep, doesn't it?

Gig bags can render a guitar easily stowable and readily portable, too, although the level of protection they offer is arguably slightly less. Make sure that you pick one that is at very least man enough to prevent nicks and dings from the day-to-day rough and tumble of life in a bluesman's arms.

If you have to travel to a gig by plane, you'll need a weapons-grade flight case which has been built to withstand the loving caress of airport baggage handlers. Having said that, I know a lot of people who have risked more flimsy cases and have never had a problem. But, statistically, it's just one of those accidents that are waiting to happen.

Of course, there are certain charmers who always manage to convince airport staff that they can take a guitar with them onboard as hand luggage, but you'd more likely end up being caught short if you relied on this all the time.

I think it's always a good plan to check with a professional guitar tech about any other precautionary pre-flight tactics. There are an awful lot of urban myths about instruments that travel the skies. Getting the real story from the people who have to clean up the mess afterwards, when an instrument has been improperly cased, is probably the best advice you'll ever have!

'When I left my covers band, telling people I wanted to play R&B, they said, "You're mad! No one wants to hear it." And I can remember saying, "You're probably right, but it's what I want to play."' *Tom McGuiness*

Gig Etiquette

Turn up on time. Essential one, this. Nothing makes me madder than hanging around waiting for musicians who have punctuality issues to address. If unavoidably detained, keep a mobile phone handy and let people know where you are well in advance of there being a serious problem.

Turning up late for even the most casual of engagements is unprofessional in the extreme and won't get you a good reputation amongst bandleaders and fellow musicians.

I've heard many bandleaders say that they'd rather

book musician A purely because he's reliable, whereas musician B is actually the better player. You figure it out...

Names And Contact Numbers

In these days of instant communication via mobile phones, email, text messages, call diverting and so on, there is really no excuse for being unavailable, and so it's a fairly easy proposition to make sure that you have the number of the venue you're playing at – and a contact name, as well. This is vital, as you never know what sort of last-minute problems are going to crop up. Make sure they have your number, too!

Soundcheck

By the time you've got to the stage where you're gigging fairly regularly with a band, soundchecks are useful for two main things: checking that your equipment is performing as you might expect it and dealing with the acoustics of the room you're playing in. In other words, make sure everything's working, set yourself a sound that you can live with, check vocal and monitor levels and leave it at that. Soundchecks are not for last-minute rehearsals – if you need that kind of thing, you're under-rehearsed and not yet ready to be allowed out in public!

Expect your guitar to sound radically different from venue to venue. Experience will teach you what works and what doesn't. If you can, move away from the stage (a long lead helps here), as sound changes as it travels. Find someone you can trust and ask them what the guitar sounds like at the back of the room.

If you're going through a PA (which is always ideal), setting the guitar sound is more straightforward because you need a good sound right in front of the amplifier as opposed to at the back of a hall or pub. Take your time here and don't get flustered. This is another good reason for turning up early.

Soundcheck vs Line Check

Here's a definition for you. Out there in pro-music land, a touring band will often not soundcheck every night. Instead, they will have a 'line check', which will usually be administered by the sound crew. This means that the guys in the crew will literally check that everything works and is making all the right noises, as opposed to the band going through the normal soundcheck ritual. A line check is usually a luxury afforded bands who are on tour and playing every night. The theory here is that sound engineers get an instinctive 'feel' for the sound of the band after a while on the road and can quite accurately predict levels and so on.

'I like playing songs like that – covers, y'know. I don't refrain from doing it for any reason other than those songs are hard to find; those special, but unusual, great songs that people haven't heard. They're really hard to find.'
Robben Ford

Being On Stage

The whole concept of being on stage is sometimes quite readily misinterpreted in the early stages of musicianship. Few realise, for instance, what an entirely different environment the live arena is to either the rehearsal room or individual practice area.

There are all sorts of additional pressures to deal with, not the least of which is the sheer fact that you're playing in front of other people! I know a good many musicians who hate playing live, but they're great musicians. They just don't like 'performing', which is an art that is way above and beyond just being able to play well.

Don't Practise On Stage

I've seen so many train wrecks on stage, where a band has obviously not rehearsed a piece well enough to perform it. If you – or anyone in the band – is at all worried about a certain song or piece, leave it back in the rehearsal room and earmark it for more work.

On a personal note, never be tempted to strike out into the unknown during a performance. Don't have a try at something you've never quite managed to pull off in rehearsal just because you're caught up in the moment, as this often leads to disaster. This is one reason why every musician will tell you that they play better when they practise; under those circumstances, they are more relaxed about experimenting, taking a few risks and so on. Playing live calls for you to play it safe for the most part.

A lot of the guys I've interviewed have the same advice to offer – and remember, these are guys at the top of their profession, so they know a thing or two. Their advice is that you've got to know what you're doing on stage to the extent that you can rely on autopilot if you're not having a good night. Obviously, autopilot means playing everything to a high standard, but possibly without those occasional sparks of creativity that turn a good performance into a memorable one.

What autopilot doesn't mean is that you've got only a 45–60 per cent chance of getting through this so please fasten your safety belts and ensure your trays are in an upright position...

Mistakes Don't Matter

What happens if you do make a mistake on stage? The best advice I can give you here is learn to laugh it off! Don't chastise yourself like an uptight tennis player; don't look up in fear at another member of the band and mouth the word 'sorry' – there's nothing to be sorry about. I've made loads of mistakes on stage (the best one being that I started to play a different number from the rest of the band one night. We were having monitoring problems and I couldn't hear properly, so I just went for what I thought the singer had announced we were going to play. Whoops!) I've seen lots of hardy pros cock things up, too – which has always had the effect of making me feel so much better.

The rest of the band might rag you about it later on, but you can bet that the mistake that you thought was as big as a mountain went unnoticed by the civilians in the audience.

Possibly the best advice here comes from Toto guitarman Steve Lukather: 'Be prepared to make mistakes because that's the way you learn; that's how you find new riffs. Just jam with your friends, make mistakes, step all over your own dick – it doesn't matter. Just have fun, go out and play, have a few beers. It doesn't matter.'

Don't Turn Your Back On The Audience

I don't want to actively encourage you to go and try out a few poses and grimaces in front of a mirror to ensure that you have at least a shot at looking cool on stage – but maybe we can sort of meet halfway?

Try not to spend the entire evening looking at the floor, your shoes, that beer stain on the carpet or whatever. You don't have to make eye contact with the audience exactly, but generally looking in their direction will look a lot better from their point of view.

Try to look like you're enjoying yourself! I was horrified when I saw a video of me playing on stage – I looked so miserable and I wasn't; I was just concentrating. Have a good time – that's what playing music is all about, and the audience will pick up on the fact that the band is having fun and will want to join in.

I used to have a sign on my teaching-room wall that said, 'Smile: you're on stage!' It was there more for a prompt for me, but plenty of students saw it and remembered it.

Eye Contact

An important one, this. I've seen lots of guitarists on stage who are in their own private places and aren't obviously communicating with the rest of the band at all and it looks wrong. You don't have to stand there gazing into each other's eyes, but keeping the band in your peripheral vision is a good way of picking up on early warning signs that something's not right. Alternatively, it's also a good way of picking up on the fact that something is going right – on these occasions sometimes the old insect brain takes over and the whole band pushes together that extra ten per cent. It's an almost magical experience when this happens, and it's something you'll miss if you're there in a little cocoon with your eyes closed!

Stage Fright

I'm lucky in that I can honestly say that I've never been nervous about playing on stage and have certainly never succumbed to the type of paralysing fear that is generally known as 'stage fright'. But I've known people to be physically sick before a performance because they get so worked up about it.

The thing is, being nervous is a perfectly natural state to be in before doing anything in front of an audience, and once you realise this, it's a little easier to deal with. You can actually channel nervous energy into a positive, performance-enhancing thing; it doesn't have to be debilitating and negative at all.

I've found that I can get very excited about playing – and sometimes the effects are very similar to what I've seen in others experiencing stage fright. They pace up and down, want to be left alone, need a drink or two to steady their nerves and so on – but they're obviously having a really bad time with it.

Before a performance, I usually need some time to myself and, yes, a glass of wine does the job of taking the edge off the situation very nicely, thank you. But I generally translate what I feel as 'excitement' and not 'nerves'.

After all, what's the worst that can happen?

APPENDIX

Chord Voicings

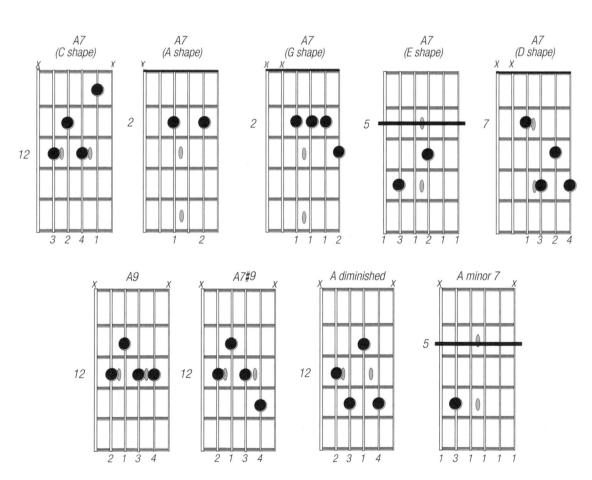

CAGED system dominant 7th chords in A

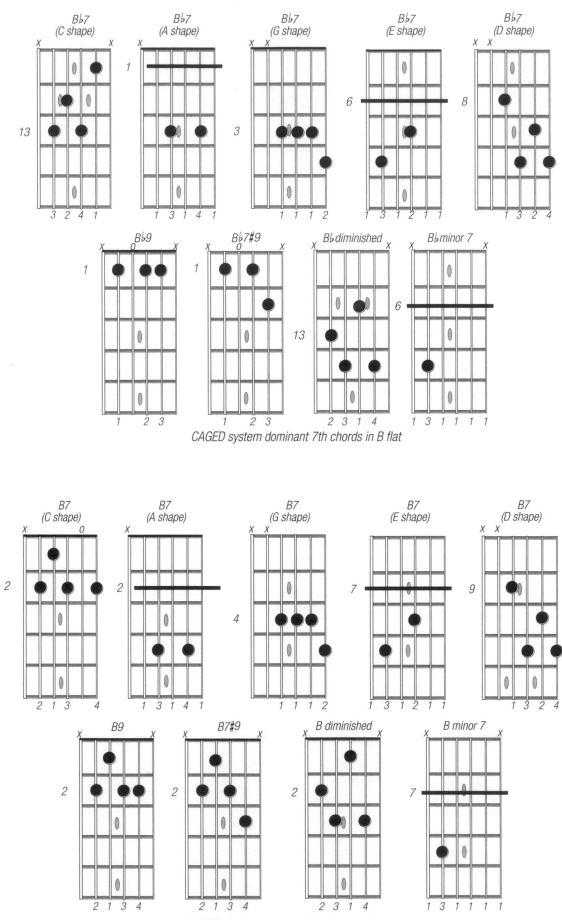

CAGED system dominant 7th chords in B flat

CAGED system dominant 7th chords in B

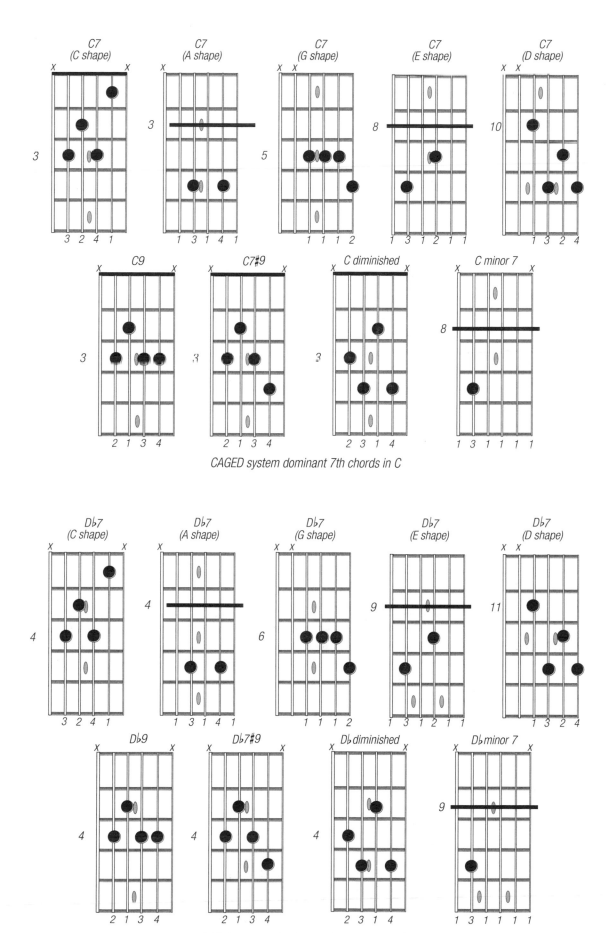

CAGED system dominant 7th chords in C

CAGED system dominant 7th chords in D flat

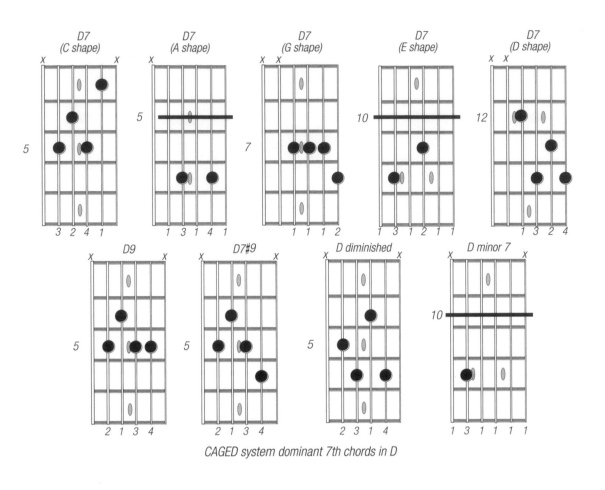

CAGED system dominant 7th chords in D

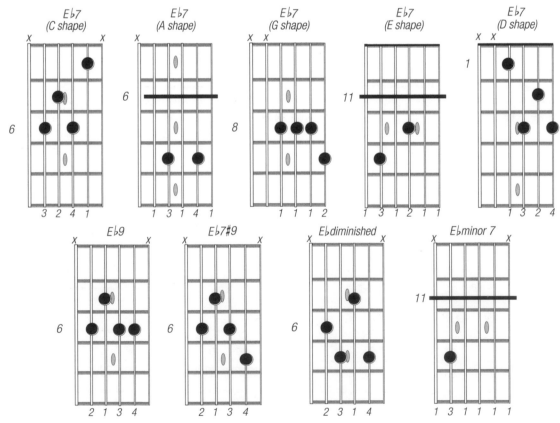

CAGED system dominant 7th chords in E flat

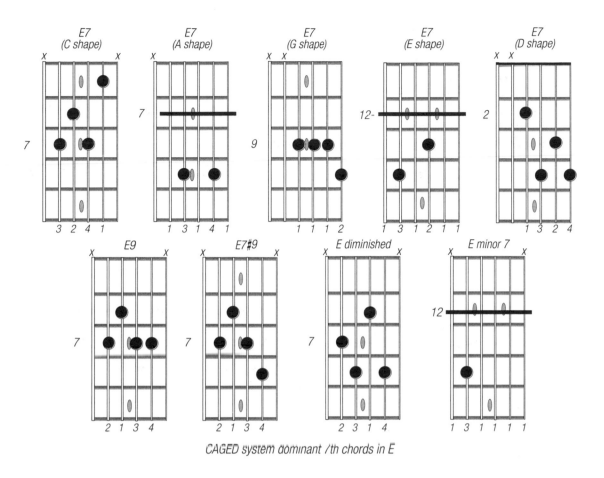

CAGED system dominant 7th chords in E

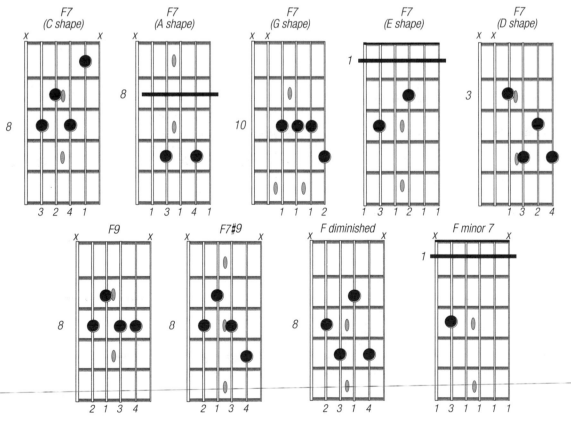

CAGED system dominant 7th chords in F

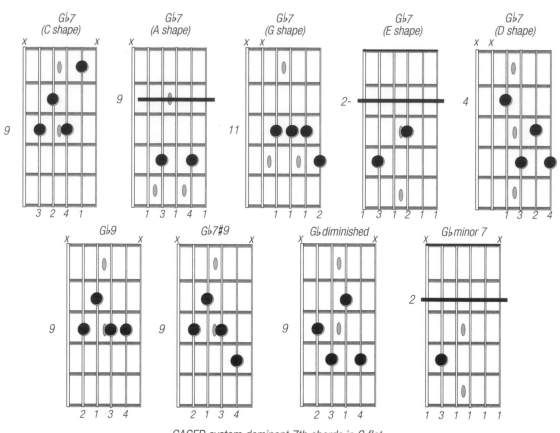

CAGED system dominant 7th chords in G flat

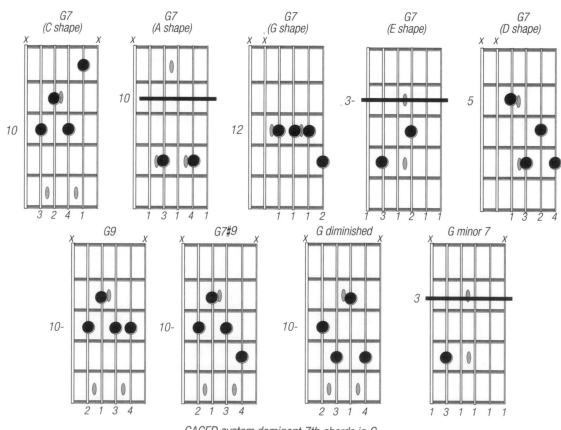

CAGED system dominant 7th chords in G

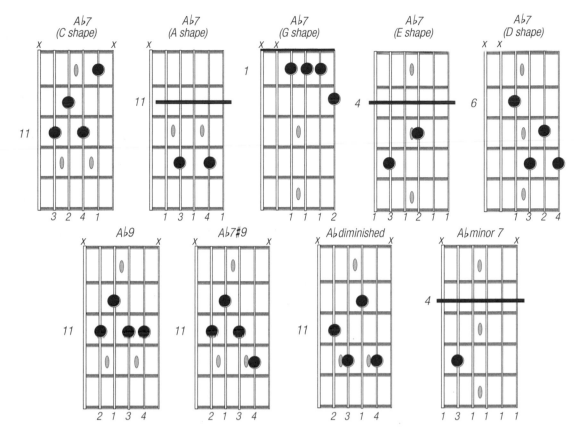

CAGED system dominant 7th chords in A flat

Scale Summary

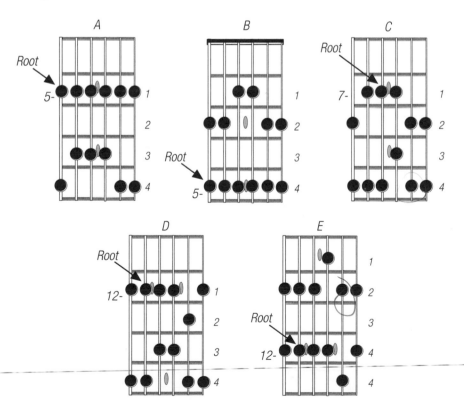

A minor pentatonic scales

A Minor Pentatonic Scales Continued

B Minor Pentatonic Scales

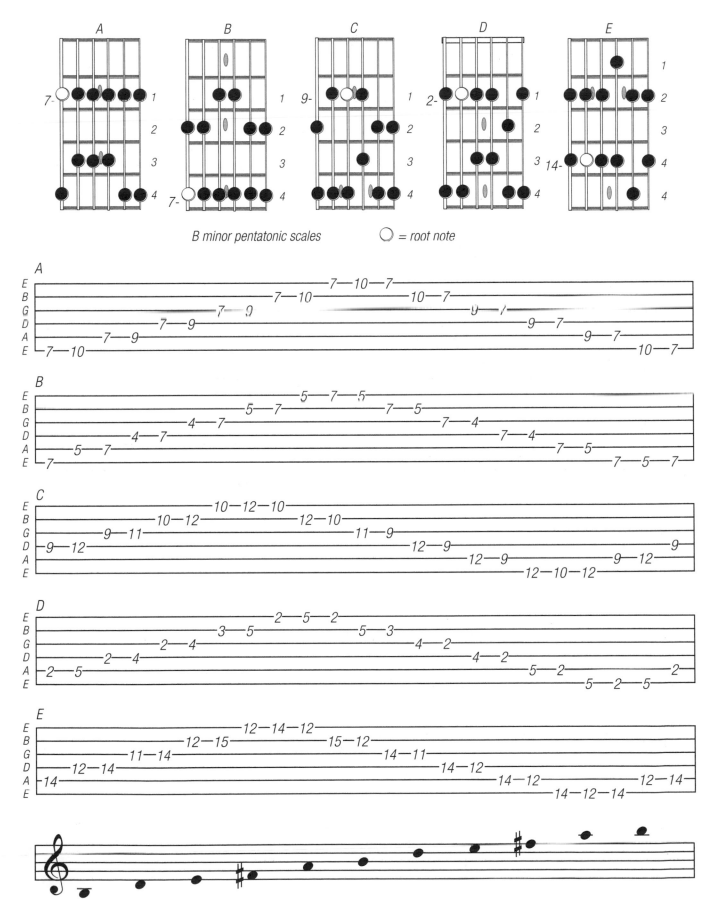

B minor pentatonic scales ○ = root note

C Minor Pentatonic Scales

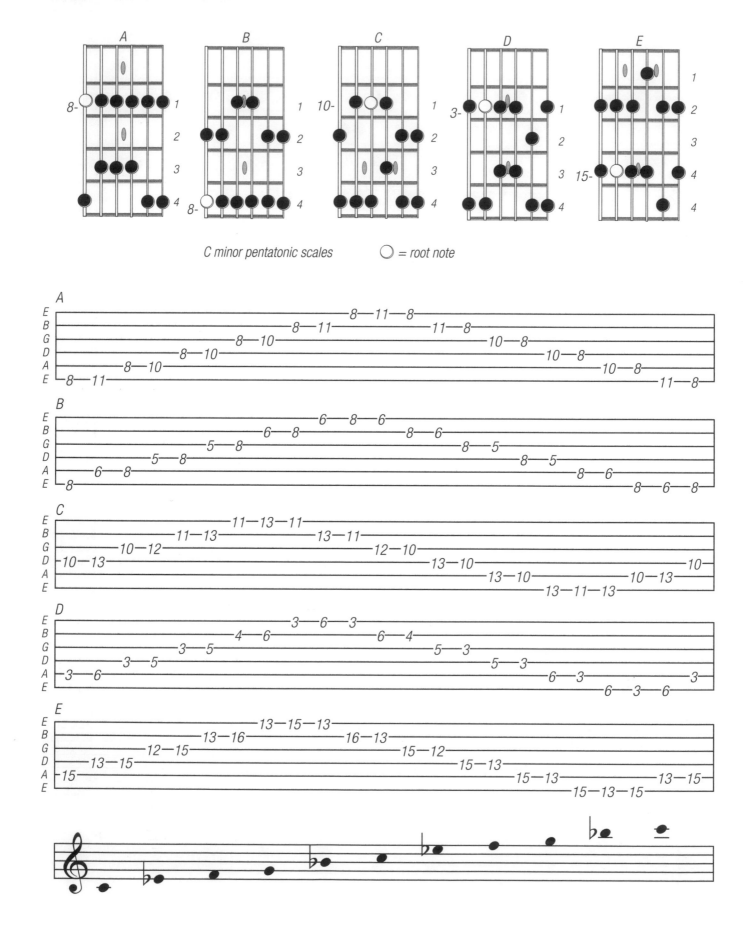

C minor pentatonic scales   ◯ = root note

D Minor Pentatonic Scales

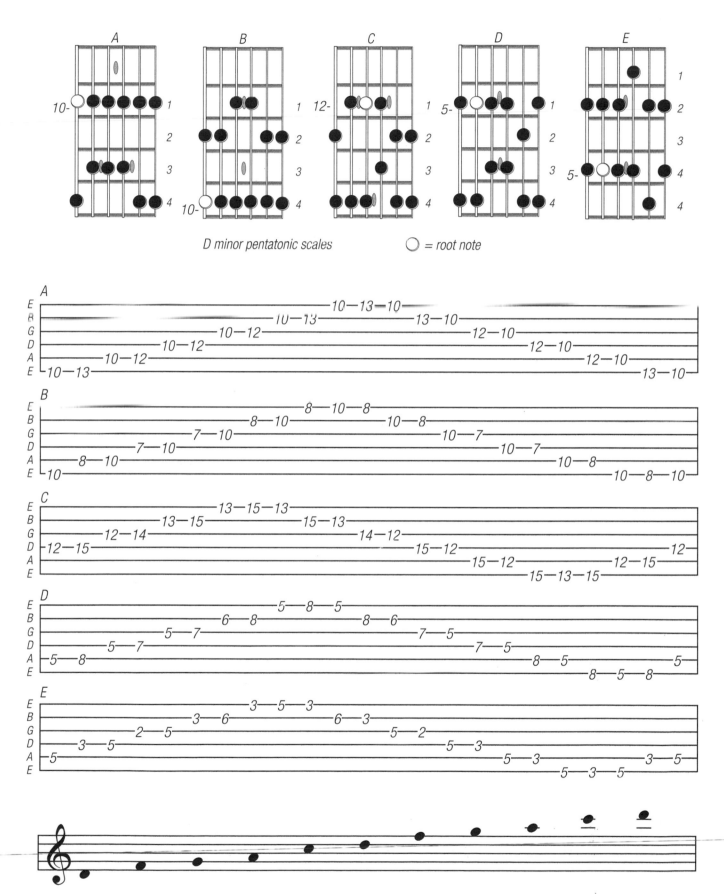

D minor pentatonic scales   ⚪ = root note

E Minor Pentatonic Scales

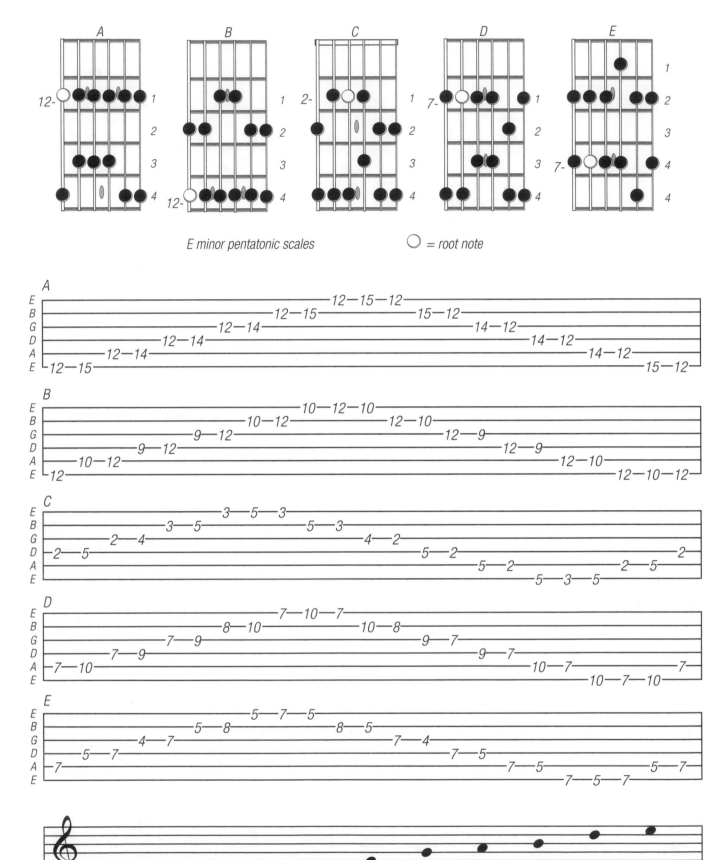

E minor pentatonic scales   ◯ = root note

F Minor Pentatonic Scales

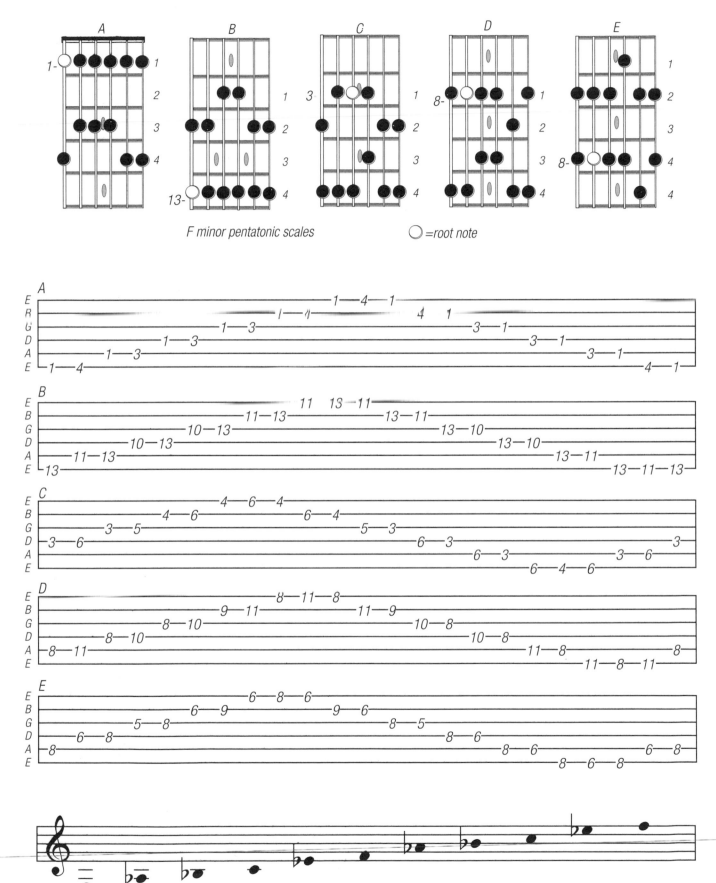

F minor pentatonic scales   ◯ =root note

G Minor Pentatonic Scales

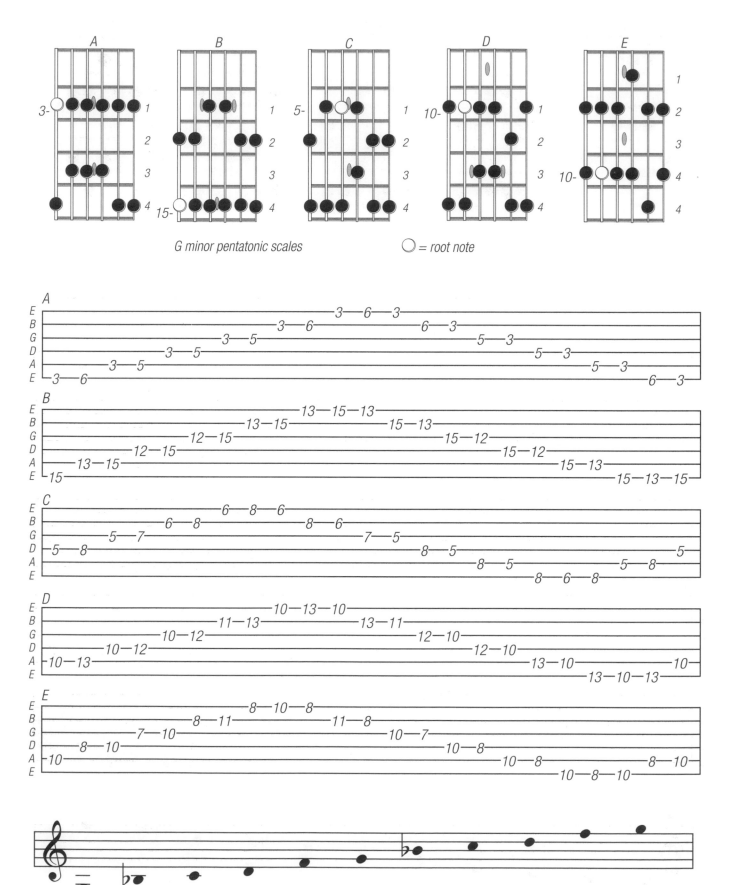

G minor pentatonic scales   ⬤ = root note

A Major Pentatonic Scales

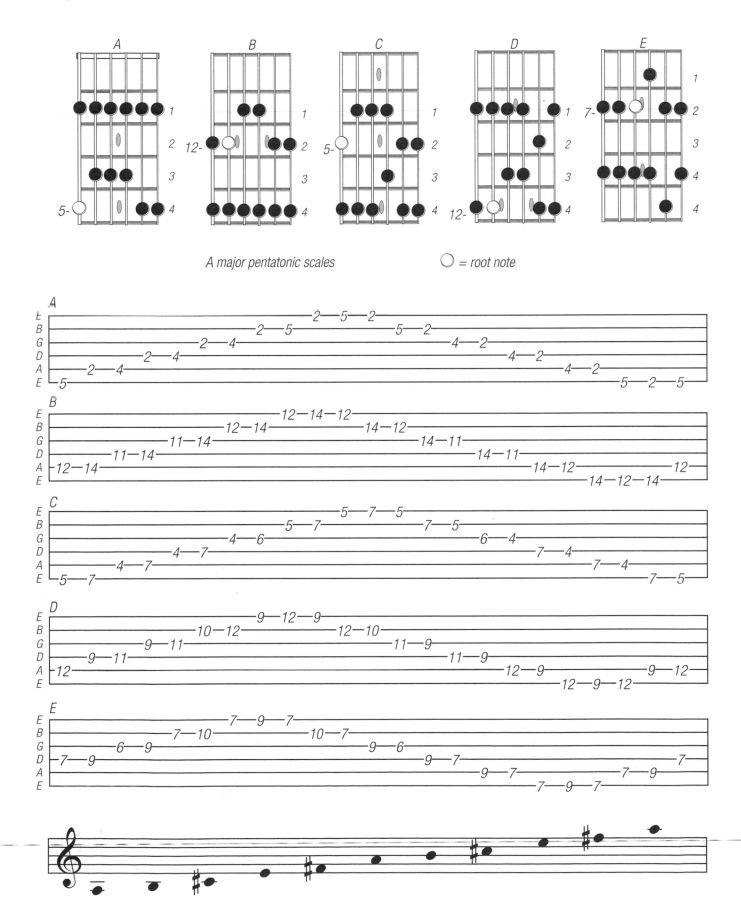

A major pentatonic scales   ⭘ = *root note*

B Major Pentatonic Scales

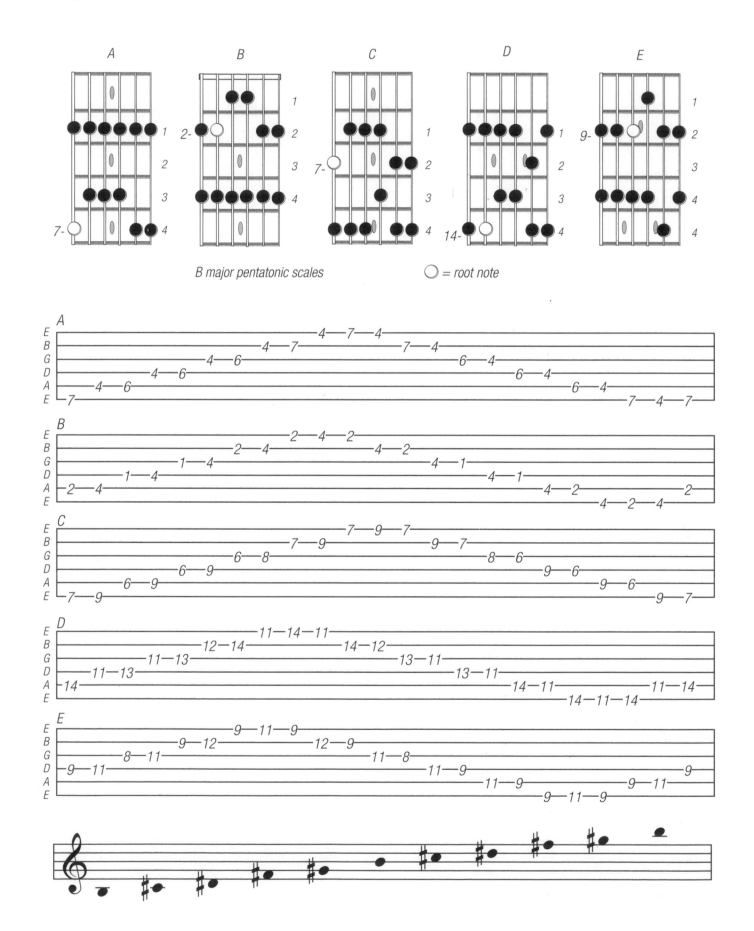

B major pentatonic scales   ◯ = root note

C Major Pentatonic Scales

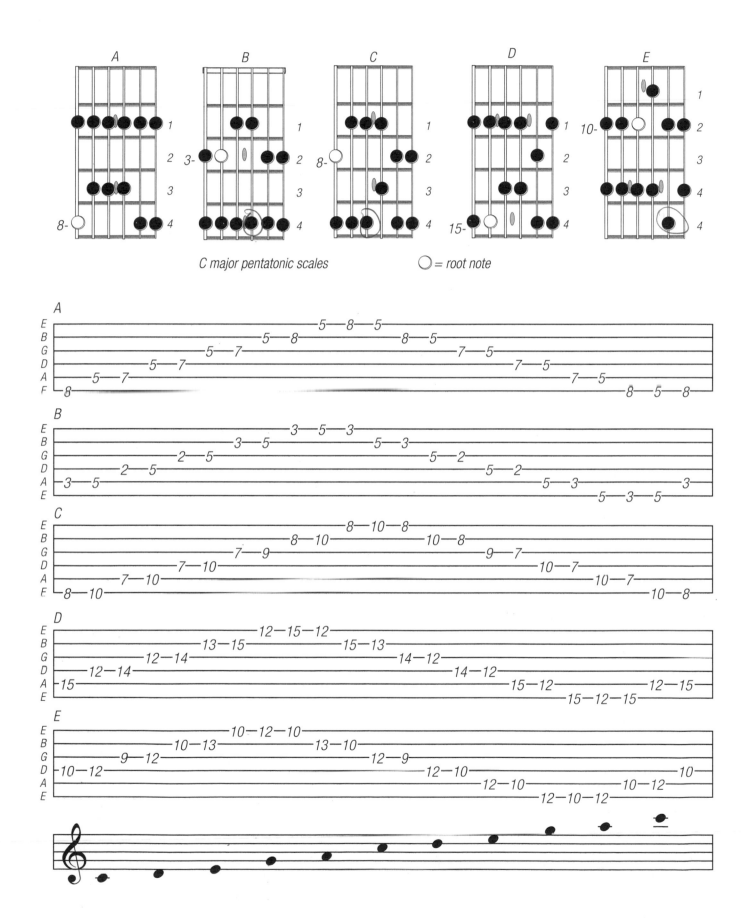

C major pentatonic scales   ◯ = root note

D Major Pentatonic Scales

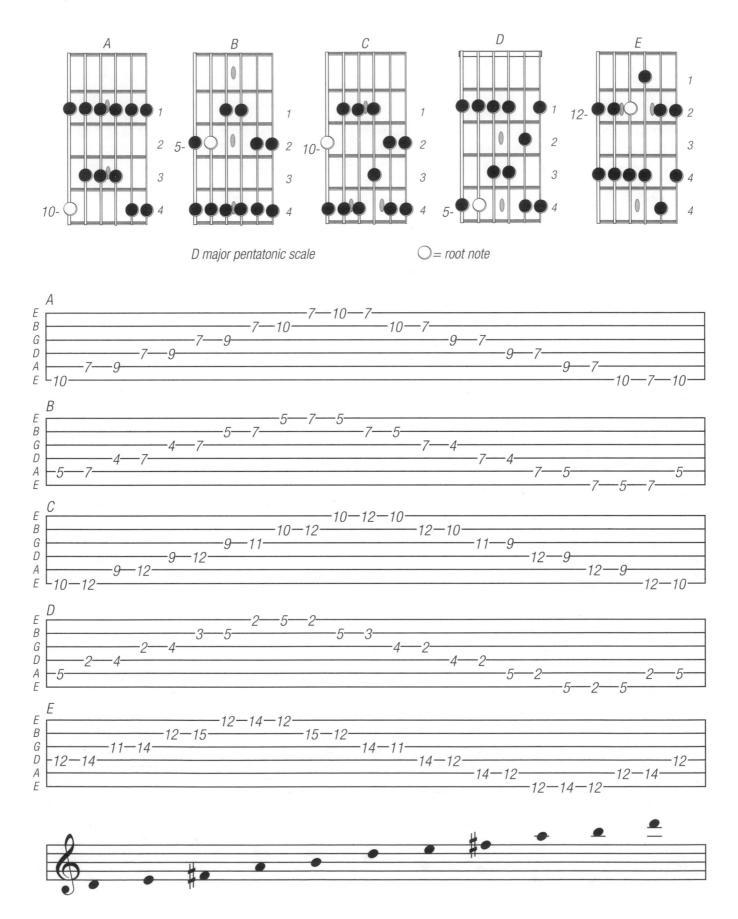

D major pentatonic scale   ○ = root note

E Major Pentatonic Scales

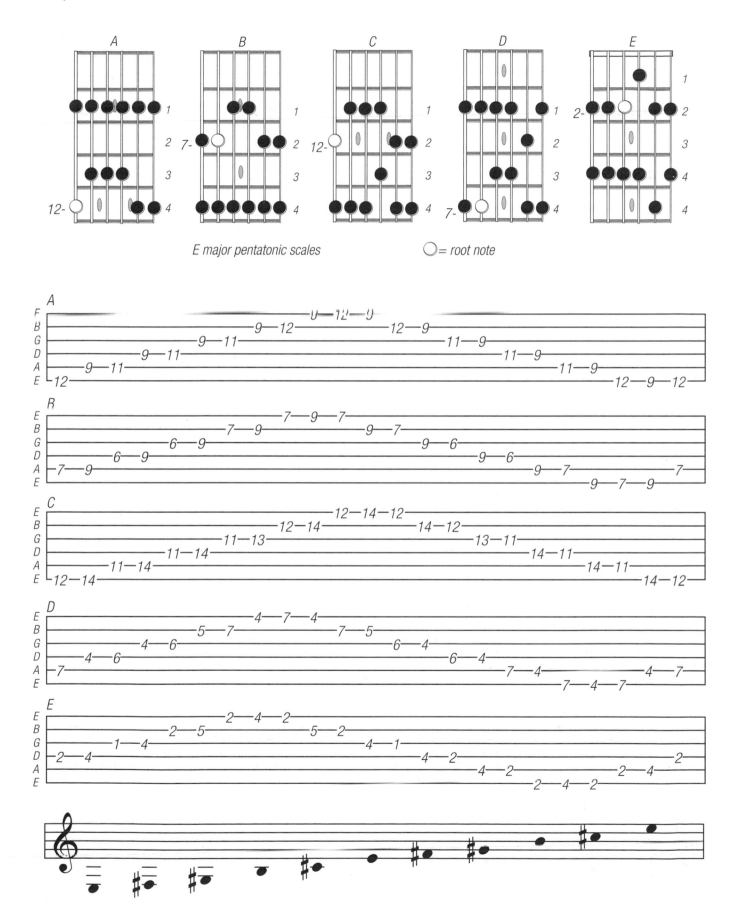

E major pentatonic scales   ◯ = root note

F Major Pentatonic Scales

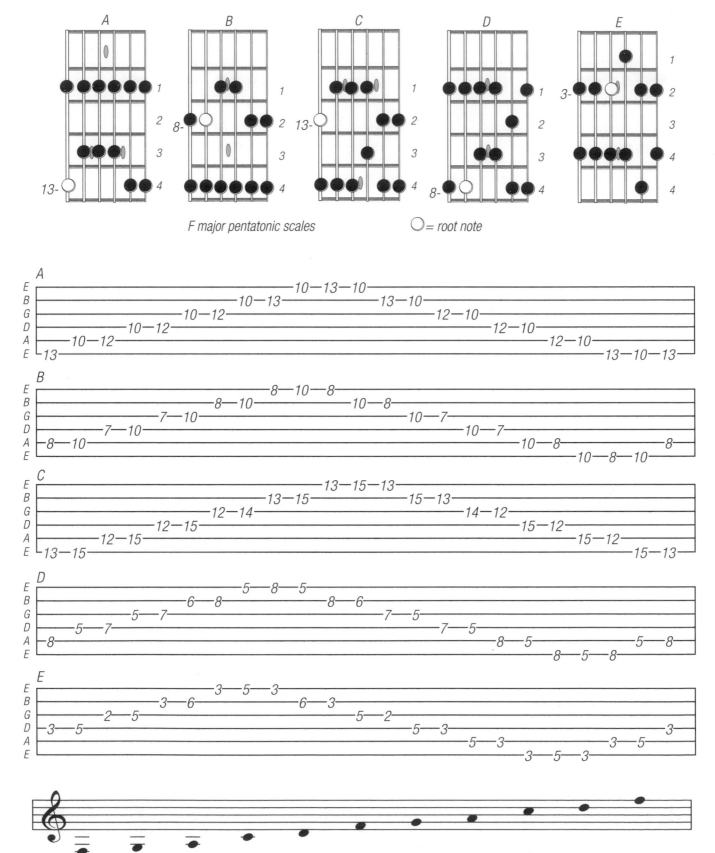

F major pentatonic scales   ◯ = root note

G Major Pentatonic Scales

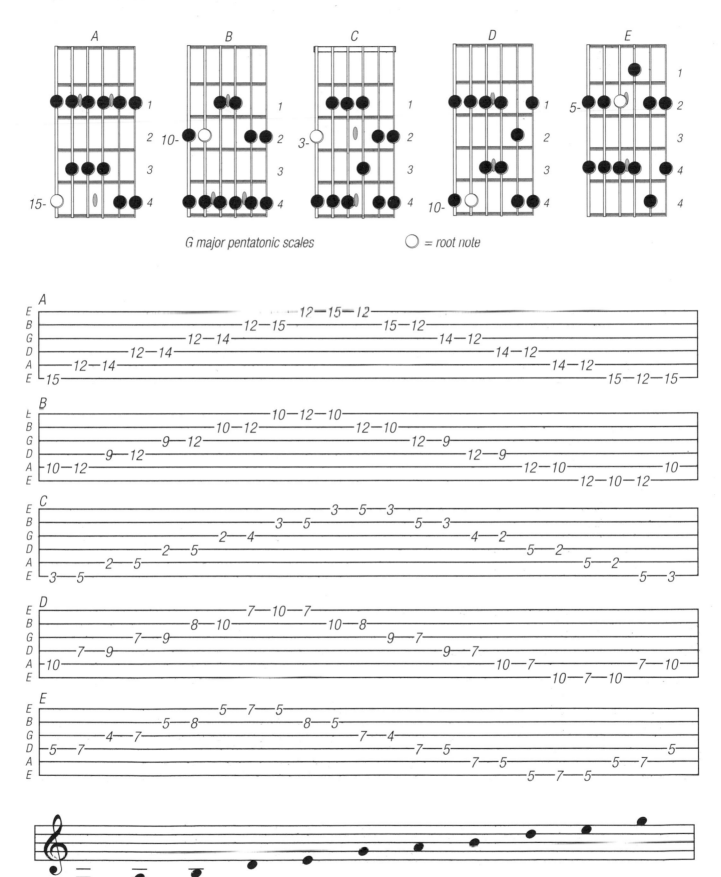

G major pentatonic scales   ◯ = root note

A Aeolian Mode/Natural Minor Scale

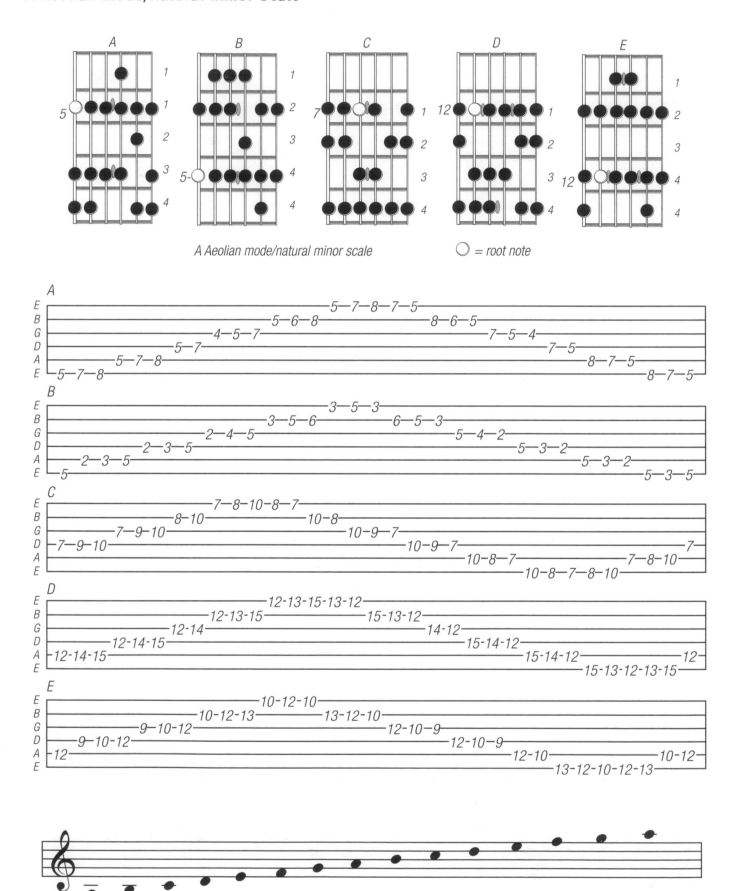

A Aeolian mode/natural minor scale   ◯ = root note

C Aeolian Mode/Natural Minor Scale

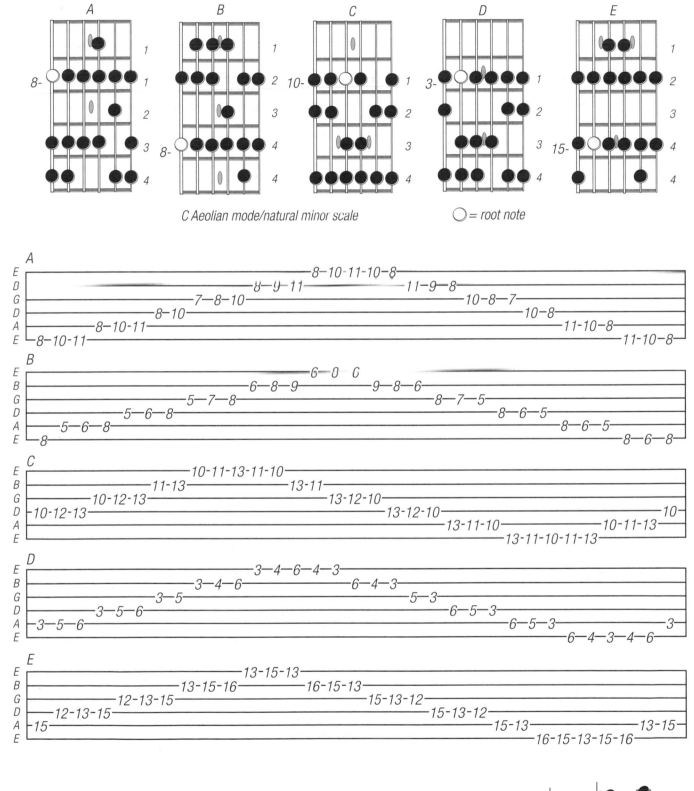

C Aeolian mode/natural minor scale   ◯ = root note

E Aeolian Mode/Natural Minor Scale

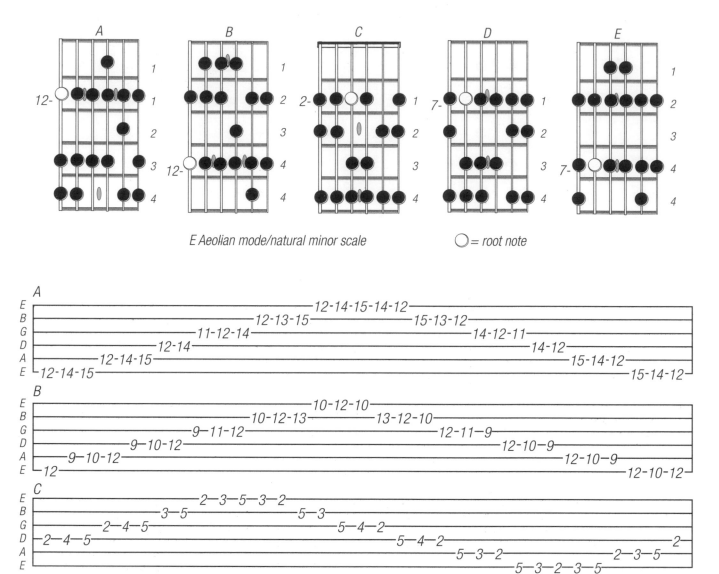

E Aeolian mode/natural minor scale   ◯ = root note

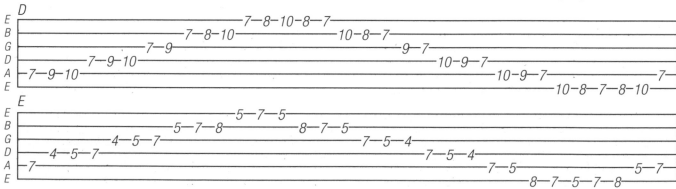

Blues Chord Charts

12-bar blues in E:

```
||: E7 / / /  | E7 / / /|  E7 / / /  | E7 / / /|
   | A7 / / /| A7 / / /  | E7 / / /|  E7 / / /  |
   | B7 / / /  | A7 / / /| E7 / / /| E7 / B7 / :||
```

12-bar blues in A:

```
||: A7 / / /  | D7 / / /   | A7 / / /| A7 / / /|
   | D7 / / /  | D7 / / /   | A7 / / /| A7 / / /|
   | E7 / / /| D7 / / /   | A7 / / /| A7 / E7 / :||
```

I–IV changes in C:

```
||: C7 / / /  | C7 / / /| C7 / / /| C7 / / /|
   | F7 / / /| F7 / / /| F7 / / /| F7 / / /|
   | C7 / / /| C7 / / /| C7 / / /| C7 / / /|
   | F7 / / /| F7 / / /| F7 / / /| F7 / / / :||
```

Riff blues in E

E riff:

A riff:

B riff:

B7#9 chord:

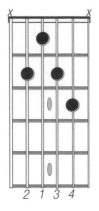

2 1 3 4

12/8 Blues In G:

‖: G7 / / / | C7 / / / | G7 / D7 / | G7 / / / |
| C7 / / / | C7 / / / | G7 / Amin7 / |
| Bmin7 / B♭min7 / | D7 / / / | D#7 / D7 / |
| G7 / C7 / | G7 / D7 / :‖

Key-Change Blues: E-F♯-A-C

E (four times)

‖: E7 / / / | A7 / / / | E7 / / / | E7 / / / |
| A7 / / / | A7 / / / | E7 / / / | E7 / / / |
| B7 / / / | A7 / / / | E7 / / / | E7 / B7 / :‖

F♯ (four times)

‖: F♯7 / / / | B7 / / / | F♯7 / / / | F♯7 / / / |
| B7 / / / | B7 / / / | F♯7 / / / | F♯7 / / / |
| C♯7 / / / | B7 / / / | F♯7 / / / | F♯ / C♯7 / :‖

A (four times)

‖: A7 / / / | D7 / / / | A7 / / / | A7 / / / |
| D7 / / / | D7 / / / | A7 / / / | A7 / / / |
| E7 / / / | D7 / / / | A7 / / / | A7 / E7 / :‖

C (four times)

‖: C7 / / / | F7 / / / | C7 / / / | C7 / / / |
| F7 / / / | F7 / / / | C7 / / / | C7 / / / |
| G7 / / / | F7 / / / | C7 / / / | C7 / G7 / :‖

Eight-Bar 'Song-Form' G Blues With Chorus:
Verse:

‖ G / / / | G7 / / / | C7 / / / | Cmin / / / |
| G7 / E7 / | A7 / D7 / | G7 / C7 / | G7 / D7 / |
| G / / / | G7 / / / | C7 / / / | C min / / / |
| G7 / E7 / | A7 / D7 / | G7 / C7 / | G7 / D7 / ‖

Chorus:

‖ C7 / / / | C min / / / | G / / / | G7 / / / |
| A / / / | A7 / / / | D7 / / / | D7 / / /‖

Verse:

‖ G / / / | G7 / / / | C7 / / / | Cmin / / / |
| G7 / E7 / | A7 / D7 / | G / C / | G / D7 / ‖

'One To Five' Eight-Bar Blues:

‖ C7 / / / | G7 / / / | F7 / / / | F♯°7 / / / |
| C7 / / / | G7 / / / | C7 / / / | C7 / G7 / ‖

12/8 Minor Blues In C:

‖ Cmin / / / | Fmin / / / | Cmin / / / |
| Cmin / / / | Fmin / / / | Fmin / / / | Cmin / / / |
| Cmin / / / | G7 / / / | Fmin / / / | Cmin / Fmin / |
| Cmin / G7 / ‖

Jazz blues in B♭:

‖ B♭ / / / | Amin7 / D7 / |
Gmin7 / C7 /	Fmin7 / B♭7 /
E♭ / / /	E♭min7 / / /	Dmin7 / / /	G7 / / /
Cmin7 / / /	F7 / / /
B♭ / Gmin7 /	Cmin7 / F7 / ‖

Accompaniment Ideas

On the CD, I've recorded a series of fingerpicked blues phrases (that can be adapted, of course, for use with a plectrum, should you prefer to use one) and embroidered them neatly together to form a little instrumental that will serve either as an accompaniment for you to play over or as part of a stand-alone blues tune in its own right.

Let's have a look at it section by section and see what we can do with them.

The first example is a slight variation on the accepted norm; we've met this phrase a few times before, but possibly not played in quite this way. John Lee Hooker in particular used to be so heavy-handed with this lick that you could often hear his strings go out of tune as he played it. (If you hit a perfectly in-tune guitar string too hard it will sound as though it's actually out of tune – it's all down to physics and so we possibly shouldn't even try to understand the reasons behind it!)

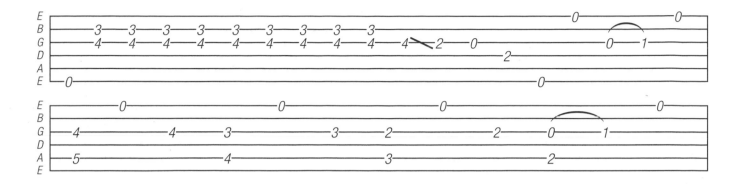

The next example demonstrates the idea we'll be playing for the E chord, harmonised for added interest.

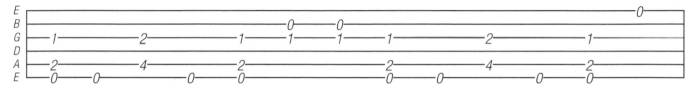

Next, the A chord motif. The harmony is similar to that of the E chord.

Finally, the B7 chord, complete with the idea of sliding the chord up a fret, momentarily entering a C7.

This is a turnaround idea that sits nicely at the end of the blues piece. It's probably the most challenging thing about this blues from a technical point of view as it calls on you to move parallel sixths together over two sets of strings (see tab). Take your time with it and don't allow yourself to become frustrated if everything keeps falling apart the first few times you try it – you'll get there in the end!

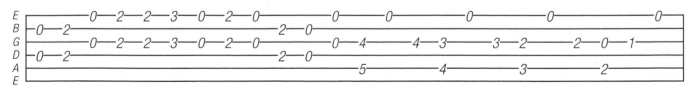

The next example incorporates all of the ideas we've looked at so far with a couple of variations thrown in for good measure. This really is a kitchen-sink blues because I threw in everything I could think of when I was recording it. Note how I keep referring back to the intro idea between chords; this is a great thing to do as a form of self-accompaniment. If there are any problems to be confronted within this blues, as far as those of us who are going to fingerpick are concerned, it will be down to things like the independence of the thumb when it plays in counterpoint to the rest of the fingers. But it's nothing that practice won't sort out.